THE POETIC SCRIPTURES OF JOHN

THE POETIC SCRIPTURES OF JOHN
GOD'S WORD IN RHYTHM & RHYME

MICHAEL D. WESTER

LIGHTHOUSE PUBLICATION
SPREADING THE WORD OF GOD, ONE BOOK AT A TIME.

Copyright © 2019 by Michael D. Wester.

All rights reserved. No part of this publication may be reproduced, distributed, or transmitted in any form or by any means, including photocopying, recording, or other electronic or mechanical methods, without the prior written permission of the author, except in the case of brief quotations embodied in critical reviews and certain other noncommercial uses permitted by copyright law.

Printed in the United States of America
ISBN 978-1-64133-625-3 (sc)
ISBN 978-1-64133-626-0 (hc)
ISBN 978-1-64133-627-7 (e)

Library of Congress Control Number: 2019917228

Artwork and Cover Design by **Cameron Klingenberg**

Inspirational / Worship and Devotion / Non-Fiction
19.11.15

Lighthouse Publication
1553 E. Caro Road
Caro, MI 48723

www.lighthousepublication.com

CONTENTS

Introduction vii

The Poetic Gospel of John 1

The Poetic Letters of John 133

    First John 133

    Second John 153

    Third John 156

The Poetic Revelation to John 159

Endnotes 243

INTRODUCTION

It was on a spring night that an overwhelming thought consumed me. Sleep escaped me as my mind flooded with unending possibilities.

As was my nightly tradition, I had gone to say good night to my teenage son. A piece of paper on his night stand caught my attention. It was a quatrain about the suffering of Christ. "Did you write this?" I asked.

"Yes," he explained. "My school assignment was to take these words and put them into the form of a rhyming poem." The words in rhyme so touched me that I urged him to put John 3:16 to rhyme.

I went to bed pondering his poem. I wondered why the rhythm and rhyme of the words so deeply impacted me. Then an idea invaded my mind. What if the whole gospel of John were put to rhyme? Would this help people focus on the truths of Scripture? Would this help people remember the events?

That night sparked the beginning of a great project of putting into rhyme all the Scriptures that John wrote. My aim has been to reflect the original meaning of Scripture as much as possible, consulting the original Greek and various translations. Because of the difficulties of this rhyming project, I found myself on occasion having to depart from the original Scriptures. Sometimes I elaborated on a meaning of a word or phrase. Other times I derived information from another place in the Bible. On occasion I repeated a phrase. Any major departure from the original Scriptures is marked by an asterisk (*).

I assigned several pastors and Bible scholars various portions of this work for their review. I thank each one for taking the time to review the theological and biblical accuracy of this work. I also thank my sister, Cam, for checking the spelling and grammar. A special thanks goes to my wife, Donna, and my two children, Josh and Sarah, for supporting me and helping me in this endeavor.

May the Lord be glorified!

THE POETIC GOSPEL OF JOHN

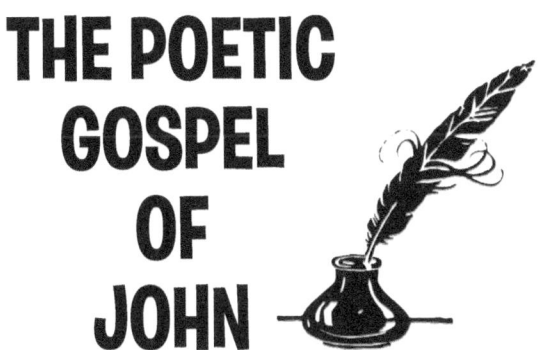

1:1   In the beginning was the Word.
       The Word was always around.
       Prior to anyone or thing,
       In God's presence He was found.

       Now this Word was not created. *
1:2   He was with God from the start,
       For as God the Word existed,
       Always with God, not apart.

1:3   Through the Word came all creation,
       Everyone and everything.
       Nothing was made apart from Him.
       By Him all came into being.

1:4   Now in the Word existed life,
       Lighting humanity.
       The life was the light within them
       Shining so brilliantly.

1:5	The light now shines in the darkness Since the world is such a dark place, But the darkness did not conquer, For the light has shown its face.[1]
1:6	God sent the world a messenger. John the Baptist was his name.
1:7	He preached about faith in the light, The reason for which he came.
1:8	Now he himself was not that light, But told all whom he could find
1:9	That the true Light comes to the world To restore light to mankind.
1:10	The true Light was already here As John preached to and fro, And though the true Light made the world, That Light they did not know.
1:11	To His own people this One came, Yet they welcomed not the Light, But to all who did receive Him, He granted the highest right.
1:12	They'd be born as God's own children, Those who in His name trust, Not children through any bloodline Or children through fleshly lust.
1:13	They'd be born as God's own children And this by one way still, Not born through a human father, But children through God's will.

1:14	Now the Word became a human.
	Among us He walked and dwelled,
	And we have viewed His glory.
	His glory we have beheld.
	His glory comes from the Father,
	Who brought Him into this place,
	And He is God's one and only,
	Being full of truth and grace.
1:15	Concerning this Word and true Light,
	John the Baptist did testify.
	In his prophetic voice he said
	These words with a mighty cry:
	"This is the One of whom I said,
	'There's One coming after me.
	He is of greater importance,
	For He has priority.'"
1:16	For from His fullness we've received
	As upon us grace He poured,
1:17	For through Moses the Law was given,
	Grace and truth through Christ the Lord.[2]
1:18	Nobody has really seen God,
	But the unique God,[3] the Word,
	Who's intertwined with the Father
	Has revealed Him.*Be assured.

The Poetic Scriptures of John

1:19	This account is John the Baptist's
	When Jerusalem Jews assigned
	Priests and Levites to question him,
	John's identity to find.
1:20	"Just who are you?" they asked bluntly.
	He answered, "The Christ I'm not."
1:21	They asked, "Then are you Elijah?"
	"No!" was the word they got.
	"Are you the Prophet, like Moses?"
	"I am not," was his reply.
1:22	"We need to report who you are,
	So we can go testify."
1:23	"Isaiah the prophet tells you,
	I'm a voice that can't be ignored,
	The voice that cries in the desert,
	'Prepare the way for the Lord.'"
1:24	The Pharisees had sent this group
1:25	Asking, "Why do you then baptize
	Since you aren't Christ or Elijah
	Or the Prophet that some surmise?"
1:26	John said, "I baptize in water,
	But there's One who is standing by.
1:27	You don't know Him. He succeeds me.
	His sandal I'm not fit to untie."

1:28	This all took place near a village—
	Bethany, *a town of small size,
	Located beyond the Jordan,
	The river where John would baptize.
1:29	On the next day John saw Jesus
	Walking over to Him.
	John said, "Behold the Lamb of God
	Who takes away the world's sin!
1:30	"This is the One of whom I said,
	'A man is coming after me.
	He is of greater importance,
	For He has priority.'
1:31	"Now I did not recognize Him,
	But Him God was to unveil.4
	That is why I came baptizing,
	To show Him to Israel."
1:32	John the Baptist then testified,
	"I saw the Spirit as a dove
	Descend upon Him and remain.
	The Spirit came from above.
1:33	"Now as I was saying before,
	Him I did not recognize,
	But I was told how I would know
	By Him who sent me to baptize.
	"'When you see the Spirit descend
	And stay upon anyone,
	That One baptizes in the Spirit.'
1:34	I tell you, this is God's Son."5

1:35	The very next day John noticed
	Jesus walking abroad.
	He told two disciples with him,
1:36	"Look! That's the Lamb of God."
1:37	The two disciples who heard this,
	To follow Him they desired.
1:38	He turned and saw them following.
	"What do you seek?" He inquired.
	They said, "Rabbi," which means teacher,
	"Tell us Your heading, we pray."
1:39	Jesus said, "Come! And you will see."
	So they stayed with Him that day.
	It was relatively early
	When they came to His abode.
	'Twas ten o'clock in the morning
	According to Roman time mode.[6]
1:40	Now one of these two disciples,
	Peter's brother Andrew,
1:41	Found his brother Simon Peter
	And gave him his review.
	"We have found the one Messiah."
	(Christ is the Greek translation.)
1:42	Andrew brought Simon to Jesus
	Who gave this proclamation:
	"You are Simon, the son of John.
	By Cephas you will be known."
	(Cephas is Hebrew for Peter,
	Which names mean rock or stone.)[7]

1:43	The next day Jesus intended To travel to Galilee. While He traveled He found Philip And commanded, "Follow Me!"
1:44	Now Philip was from Bethsaida, Where Andrew and Peter were from.
1:45	Philip went and found Nathanael, And said to persuade him to come: "The One about whom Moses wrote, We have found Him, the Promised One,[8] Of whom the Prophets also wrote, Jesus of Nazareth, Joseph's son."
1:46	But with doubt Nathanael replied, "Can any good come from there, That despised place of Nazareth?" "Come and see!" was Philip's dare.
1:47	Jesus saw Nathanael coming, And him He did applaud. "Look! A genuine Israelite In whom there is no fraud!"
1:48	Nathanael replied to Jesus, "Where did You come to know me?" He said, "Before Philip called you, I saw you under the fig tree."
1:49	Nathanael responded, "Rabbi! You most certainly are God's Son. You are the King of Israel. You are the Promised One!"

1:50	Jesus answered, "Because I said I saw you under the fig tree, Do you have faith now to believe? You'll see greater things of Me.
1:51	"Truly, truly, you will witness Heaven with an open span, God's angels going up and down[9] Upon the Son of Man!"

2:1	The third day of Jesus's travels In Cana of Galilee, His mother was at a wedding, And there Jesus went to be.
2:2	For Jesus and His disciples Were invited to this feast. As all the people celebrated,
2:3	The wine eventually ceased.
	Mary reported to Jesus, "The servants say there's no wine!"
2:4	"Dear lady," He kindly stated, "This problem is not Mine.
	"My hour has not yet arrived To be in the open view."
2:5	Then Mary ordered the servants, "Whatever He says, you do."

2:6   Now there were six stone water pots.
Each was set for dispensing
From twenty to thirty gallons
For ceremonial cleansing.

2:7   "Get more water and fill them up,"
The servants were ordered by Him.
They did as Jesus demanded,
Filling the vessels to the brim.

2:8   "Now draw some of the water out,"
The servants He commanded,
"And take it to the headwaiter."
They did as He demanded.

2:9   Now Jesus did a miracle.
He turned water into wine.
When the headwaiter tasted it,
He knew it was very fine.

He did not know from where it came,
Though the servants knew full well.
So he called over the bridegroom
For a compliment to tell.

2:10   "Every groom serves the good wine first,
And when all have had their fill,
The lesser wine he then brings out,
But you have the good wine still!"

2:11   This was Jesus's first miracle
In Cana of Galilee.
His disciples put their faith in Him
Since His glory they could see.

2:12	He then went down to Capernaum With His mother and brothers too And also with His disciples. The days they stayed were few.
2:13	Since the Jewish celebration Called Passover was at hand, Up to Jerusalem He went. To enter the temple He planned.
2:14	When He entered into the court, This is how He was greeted: With oxen, sheep, and dove sellers, And moneychangers seated.
2:15	He made a whip out of small rope And forced the people out Along with the sheep and oxen, And He scattered their coins about.
	Jesus overturned their tables.
2:16	To those selling doves He said, "Remove these from My Father's house. Don't make it a market instead."
2:17	His disciples were there with Him As they witnessed this ordeal. They remembered it was written, "Your house will fill Me with zeal."
2:18	The Jews approached Jesus and asked, "What gives You the authority To do these things in this temple? What sign will You have us see?"

2:19	"If you all destroy this temple, In just three days you would see That I Myself will restore it," He answered fearlessly.
2:20	The Jews replied, "Impossible! It took forty-six years to raise! Are You so arrogant to think That You can build it in days?"
2:21	Now Jesus did not mean at all The temple of which they said But the temple of His body That He would raise from the dead.
2:22	His disciples later recalled this After He was raised from the dead. Then they believed the Scriptures And the words that Jesus said.
2:23	When He was in Jerusalem During the Passover feast, Many believed in the Lord's name As His miracles increased.
2:24	But He did not entrust Himself To those at the Jewish feast Since He understood every man From the greatest to the least.
2:25	He did not need to hear from men For Him to understand. He understood for He could see The heart of every man.

The Poetic Scriptures of John

3:1 There was a ruler of the Jews.
To Jesus at night he came.
He also was a Pharisee.
Nicodemus was his name.

3:2 "Rabbi, we of the council know
You're God's teacher in these times
Because unless God were with You,
You could not perform these signs."

3:3 Jesus said to Nicodemus,
"I speak the truth to you.
Nobody can see God's kingdom
Unless he is born anew."[10]

3:4 "How can one be born when he's old?"
Nicodemus began to chime.
"He can't enter his mother's womb
And be born a second time!"

3:5 "This is the truth of God's kingdom,"
Jesus explained to him,
"Without being born of water and Spirit,
No one can enter in.

3:6 "For when one is born from the flesh,
The result is physical.
When one is born from the Spirit,
The result is spiritual.

3:7	"Do not marvel because I said You have to be born anew. Listen to this deep mystery From the wind that just came through.[11]
3:8	"You hear the wind blow where it wills, Yet don't know from where it came, And you don't know where it's going. Spiritual birth is the same."
3:9	Nicodemus still was puzzled. He asked, "How can this be?"
3:10	Jesus said, "You're Israel's teacher, And still you do not see?
3:11	"Why can't you understand these things? Why can't you just believe? We teach and testify of truth,[12] Yet our words you don't receive.
3:12	"Since you don't accept My teachings By analogy from this earth, How will you believe My teachings Of things like heavenly birth?
3:13	"Now no one has been in heaven, That is, no one other than He who has come down from heaven, The One called the Son of Man.
3:14	"As Moses in the wilderness Raised up the brazen snake, So also must the Son of Man Be raised up on a stake.

3:15	"So that anyone who has faith, Anyone who does believe, Relying on the Son of Man, Eternal life he'll receive.
3:16	"For God did love the world this way: His only[13] Son He gave That whoever believes in Him, Forever from death He'll save.
3:17	"For God sent not His only Son To condemn the world for sin, But God did send His only Son To save the world through Him.
3:18	"He who trusts in Him is not judged, But judgment has already come On him who trusts not in the name Of God's one and only Son.
3:19	"This is the basis of judgment: Into the world came the light, But men loved the darkness instead, Not wanting to do what's right.
3:20	"For those who practice evil deeds Hate the light and do not care. They do not come into the light So their deeds are not laid bare.
3:21	"But he who practices the truth, To the light he draws near So that his deeds are done through God. In the light his deeds appear."

3:22	After leaving Jerusalem,
	In Judea He did arise,
	Spending time with His disciples,
	And there He did baptize.
3:23	There was much water in Aenon.
	Salim, this place was near.
	So John was also baptizing
	Since many were coming here.
3:24	John had not yet been imprisoned
3:25	When there was deliberation
	By his disciples with a Jew
	About purification.
3:26	They came to John saying, "Rabbi,
	This news we now deliver
	Concerning Him who was with you
	Beyond the Jordan River.
	"This One whom you had testified
	Would take away the world's sin,
	Look! He is also baptizing,
	And all are coming to Him!"
3:27	John replied to his disciples,
	"Nothing can one receive
	Unless from heaven it's been given.
	This you must believe.*

3:28	"Remember what I testified: 'The Christ I myself am not, But I was sent ahead of Him.' Remember what I have taught.
3:29	"A bride belongs to the bridegroom. His friend listens for his voice. He's very glad when he hears it. So I exult and rejoice!
3:30	"He must become more visible, But I am to diminish. His ministry must continue While mine I am to finish.
3:31	"He comes from heaven. I'm from earth. To earth my speech is confined. So because He comes from heaven, He is above all mankind.
3:32	"He speaks of what He's seen and heard, But those who receive are few.
3:33	I who have received His witness Testify that God is true.
3:34	"For whom God sent declares God's words. He only speaks God's pleasure, For God has poured upon this One The Spirit without measure.
3:35	"The Father loves His only Son, Placing all things in His hand.
3:36	Whoever believes in the Son Has eternal life, *understand.

"But the one who does not believe
In the Son, whom must be obeyed,
Will not be able to see life,
But on him God's wrath has stayed."

4:1   Reports had reached the Pharisees
That Jesus was outdoing John
By baptizing much more people.
More disciples He had drawn.

4:2   Yet Jesus was not baptizing.
This His disciples would do.
Knowing the Pharisees had heard,
4:3   From Judea He withdrew.

He headed back to Galilee.
4:4   Through Samaria He went.
Jews normally went around it,[14]
But He could not circumvent.

4:5   He came to the city Sychar.
Near a piece of land it lay
That Jacob gave his son Joseph
Before death could have its way.[15]

4:6   Now Jacob's well was also there,
And Jesus, being worn out,
Was resting from His journey there.
It was six o'clock about.[16]

4:7	A woman of Samaria
	Came to draw some water there.
4:8	His disciples were in Sychar
	Purchasing some food to share.

"Give Me a drink," He said to her.
4:9 She replied, "You are a Jew!
Why ask me? I'm Samaritan,
And I'm a woman too."

As for Jews and Samaritans,
They do not associate.
They don't deal with one another.
Their relationship is hate.

4:10 Jesus said, "If you knew God's gift,
And the One who has been speaking,
The One who asked you for a drink,
From Him you would be seeking.

"If you had asked Him for a drink,
Living water He'd be giving."
4:11 The woman did not understand
This thought of water living.

She said to Him, "Please tell me, sir,
Will You get this water here?
You have nothing with which to draw,
And the well is too deep I fear.

4:12 "Our father Jacob gave us this.
From the well he would drink,
Also his sons and his cattle.
Are You greater, do You think?"

4:13	He said, "Those who drink this water
	Will thirst for more now and then,
4:14	But whoever drinks My water,
	He will never thirst again.

        "The water that I give to him
        Will be a perpetual spring
        Filled up with water all the time,
        Eternal life to bring."

4:15	She asked, "Oh sir, please give to me
	This water of which You tell
	So that I'll never thirst and need
	To draw water from this well."
4:16	"Go tell your husband to come here,"
	Jesus commanded her.
4:17	The woman answered back to Him,
	"I have no husband, sir."

        Jesus said, "You have been truthful.
        You've no husband I understand,

4:18	For you have had five of them,
	And you're now living with a man."
4:19	"You have to be a prophet, sir!
4:20	Our fathers worshipped up there,
	The mountain, not Jerusalem
	Where you Jews insist and declare."
4:21	He said to her, "Believe My words!
	For I'm making you aware
	That worshipping the Father
	Will be neither here nor there.

4:22 "You worship now in ignorance.
      With the Jews that's not the case.
      Ours is out of revelation.
      Salvation is from our race.

4:23 "Time is coming and now has come
      When true worshippers will render
      Worship to God in spirit and truth.
      To the Father they'll surrender.

4:24 "The Father seeks such worshippers
      Because a spirit is He.
      So those who worship the Father,
      In spirit and truth must be."

4:25 "I know Messiah is coming,"
      (That is, the Christ) said she,
      "Then He'll declare all things to us."
4:26 He said, "I who speak am He."

4:27 At this time His disciples came
      While with her He was speaking.
      Shocked they dared not ask Him why,
      Or what from her He was seeking.

4:28 The woman left her water pot.
      To the city she did run.
4:29 "Come see the One who told to me
      All the things which I have done.

4:30 "Could the Messiah be this Man?"
      To Christ they went to meet,
4:31 And while they made their way to Him,
      His disciples said, "Rabbi, eat."

4:32	Jesus said, "I have food to eat
	Of which you are not versed."
4:33	They were asking one another,
	"Did someone feed Him first?"
4:34	Jesus said to His disciples,
	"My food is to do His will,
	The will of Him who sent Me,
	Whose work I'm to fulfill.
4:35	"I am certain you all have said
	In four months crops will be ripe,
	But look up and see the white fields,
	A harvest of another type.
4:36	"He who reaps now receives wages.
	Eternal life's fruit he collects
	So that the joy of the sower
	And the reaper intersects.
4:37	"In this case the saying is true,
	'One person does the planting.
	Another does the harvesting.'
	So this is what I'm granting:
4:38	"I send you to reap a harvest
	For which you did not strain.
	Where other people have labored,
	You will have reaped the gain."
4:39	So in Sychar many believed
	Due to this witness of one:
	"Come see the One who told to me
	All the things which I have done."

The Poetic Scriptures of John

4:40	When the Samaritans had come,
	His stay they did implore.
	So He went into the city,
	Remaining two days more.
4:41	Now many more Samaritans
	Listened to Him and believed.
4:42	They were saying to the woman,
	"The Messiah we've received.
	"Our faith is not based on your words,
	For He opened up our mind.
	We now know that He is the One,
	The Savior of mankind."

4:43	After two more days Jesus left.
	To Galilee He did roam.
4:44	For He had said a prophet has
	No honor in his own home.
4:45	So when He came to Galilee,
	He was welcomed by everyone,
	For many had been at the feast
	And had seen the things He'd done.
4:46	Jesus went again to Cana
	Where He had made water wine.
	There was a royal official there
	Whose son was sick at that time.

4:47	When he heard that Jesus returned, He went and asked Him to come To the city of Capernaum To heal his dying son.
4:48	Jesus said, "Before believing, Signs and wonders you require."
4:49	The royal official said, "Please, sir, Come or my child will expire!"
4:50	Jesus said to the official, "Your son lives! Be on your way." Believing the word Jesus spoke, The official did obey.
4:51	On his way down to Capernaum, It was the very next day, His servants intercepted him, "Your son lives," they did say.
4:52	"Tell me when my son got better?" The father did implore. "Yesterday at seven o'clock,[17] The fever was no more."
4:53	He then recalled the time and words, "Your son lives," as Jesus told, And he himself came to believe Along with his whole household.
4:54	This is the second miracle Performed by Jesus, you see, Since coming out of Judea And into Galilee.

The Poetic Scriptures of John

5:1	Later there came a Jewish feast.
	To Jerusalem He arose
5:2	To the pool of Bethesda,
	Having five porticoes.
5:3	The pool was next to the sheep gate,
	And the needy were lying there,
	The sick, blind, the lame, and withered.
	At the water they would stare.
5:4	They were waiting for an angel
	To cause the water to stir.
	Whoever was the first one in,
	Their healing would occur.
5:5	A man, lame for thirty-eight years,
	Was waiting as all could tell.
5:6	Jesus asked, knowing his health,
	"Do you really wish to get well?"
5:7	"Sir, I have no one to help me.
	Others beat me off this dock."
5:8	He complained, but Jesus commanded,
	"Pick up your bedroll and walk."
5:9	The man was healed immediately,
	And walked, carrying his bed,
	But it was on the Sabbath day
	When he did as Jesus said.

5:10	The Jewish leaders saw the man, And began to criticize, "It's not lawful on the Sabbath To bear beds of any size."
5:11	But he said, "The Healer told me, 'Pick up your bedroll and walk.'"
5:12	So they asked him, "Who is this Man Who defies us with such talk?"
5:13	The healed man did not know His name. He only knew His face. By then Jesus had slipped away From the crowded place.
5:14	In the temple Jesus met him, And said, "You're well. Behold! Do not continue in your sin So nothing worse may unfold."
5:15	The man departed from that place, The Jewish leaders to tell. He told them that it was Jesus, The One who had made him well.
5:16	For this reason the Jews began To persecute the Lord,[18] Because such things He was doing With Sabbath rules ignored.
5:17	He'd say, "My Father always works So I must do this too."
5:18	The Jews plotted to murder Him Because their anger grew.*

> Because He broke their Sabbath rules,
> They looked at Him with hate.*
> By calling God His own Father,
> With God He did equate.

5:19
> Jesus responded to these Jews,
> "The truth I say to you.
> The Son can only work the things
> He sees the Father do.

> "For whatever the Father does,
> The Son accomplishes too.

5:20
> Because the Father loves the Son,
> He shows Him what to do.

> "And there will be much greater works
> The Son will see from God,
> And you will see all of these things
> So that you may be awed.

5:21
> "As the Father raises the dead,
> And to them life abides,
> So also the Son will give life
> To whomever He decides.

5:22
> "Judgment has been given the Son.
> With this God[19] does not bother.

5:23
> This way all may honor the Son
> As they honor the Father.

> "Whoever dishonors the Son,
> Dishonors the Father too,
> For God is the One who sent Him,
> And all that I say is true.

5:24	"Truly, truly, I say to you,
	He who hears what I say,
	Believing in Him who sent Me,
	Eternal life he has this day.
	"He who believes Him who sent Me,
	Into judgment he won't come
	Because he has passed out of death
	And into life in His Son.
5:25	"Truly, truly, I say to you,
	A time is both now and near.
	As the dead listen to God's Son,
	The dead will live who hear.
5:26	"The Father has life in Himself.
	He put life in His Son's hand.
5:27	He has authority to judge,
	For He's the Son of Man.
5:28	"For there is coming an hour,
	About this don't feel surprise,
	In which all who are in the tombs
	Will hear His voice and rise.
5:29	"Those who practiced the godly deeds,
	To life they will resurrect,
	But those who practiced the bad deeds,
	Judgment will be the effect.
5:30	"I can initiate nothing.
	I judge only as I hear,
	And the judgment I give is just.
	From His will I do not veer.

	"For I do not seek My own will.
	My Sender's will I do.
5:31	If I just attest of Myself,
	My witness would not be true.
5:32	"Someone else testifies of Me,
	Whose testimony is true.
5:33	You have sent and have questioned John.
	The truth he told to you.
5:34	"The witness I take is not from man.
	That's how I have behaved.*
	The purpose that I say these things
	Is so you may be saved.
5:35	"John was the lamp that was burning.
	He was shining by God's plan,
	And you were willing to rejoice
	In his light for a short time span.
5:36	"My witness is greater than John's,
	For what God sent Me to do,
	The very works that I practice,
	These prove He sent Me too.
5:37	"And the Father who has sent Me,
	Of Me He has testified.
	You haven't ever heard His voice.
	His form you've never eyed.
5:38	"His Word is not living in you.
	You distrust Him whom He sent.
5:39	For eternal life you search God's Word.[20]
	God's Word makes Me evident.

5:40	"You're unwilling to come to Me
	To receive life in these days.
5:41	I do not seek from any man
	Their approval or their praise.
5:42	"You do not have God's love in you,
	For your hearts I do perceive.
5:43	I have come in My Father's name,
	Yet Me you don't receive.
	"If someone else should come to you
	In his very own name,
	You willingly receive that one.
	I say this to your shame.
5:44	"You seek honor from one another
	Instead of from the one God.
	How will you then come to believe
	When you act out this façade?
5:45	"Do not think I will accuse you
	Before My Father," He stressed.
	"But Moses will accuse you all
	In whom your hope does rest.
5:46	"If you trust Moses, you'd trust Me,
	For about Me Moses wrote.
5:47	So how will you believe My words
	If you don't trust what you quote?"[21]

The Poetic Scriptures of John

6:1 Jesus went to Tiberias,
       On the far side of the sea.
6:2 A big crowd was following Him
       To this part of Galilee.

       The reason that they followed Him
       Was because they all did witness
       Jesus performing miracles,
       Ridding people of their sickness.

6:3 Jesus went up on a mountain
       As the crowd gathered here;
       He sat down with His disciples.
6:4 Now the Passover was near.

6:5 As Jesus saw the coming crowd,
       To Philip He did inquire,
       "Where are we to buy enough bread
       That this crowd does require?"

6:6 Now Jesus was testing Philip,
       Already having a plan;
6:7 "Two hundred days' wages[22] won't buy
       Even a little for each man."

6:8 "Five barley loaves and two small fish,"
6:9 Peter's brother Andrew said,
       "I got it from this little boy,
       But they still won't get fed."

6:10   Jesus said, "Have the people sit."
         For much grass was to be found.
         So the men sat down in their groups.
         Five thousand gathered around.

6:11   Jesus then took all of the loaves,
         Giving thanks in God's name;
         He gave to them all they wanted.
         With the fish He did the same.

6:12   He commanded His disciples
         After feeding the whole lot,
         "Gather all that is left over.
         To waste food we must not."

6:13   They collected the leftovers
         From the crowd whom they had fed,
         And filled twelve baskets with fragments
         From the five loaves of bread.

6:14   When the crowd saw the miracle,
         The sign which Jesus had done,
         They said, "Truly, He's the Prophet
         Who into the world has come!"

6:15   The crowd was meaning to force Him
         To be king, which Jesus knew.
         So into solitude He went.
         Up the mountain He withdrew.

The Poetic Scriptures of John

6:16	His disciples went to the sea
	When evening time had come.
6:17	They got into a boat to cross
	Over to Capernaum.
6:18	Darkness had overtaken them
	When the wind began to blow.
	Now Jesus was not with them yet,
	And it was hard to row.*
6:19	After rowing three or four miles,
	They saw one coming near
	Who was walking on the water.
	They were overcome with fear.
6:20	"Fear not! It's Me!" Jesus exclaimed,
6:21	They eagerly let Him aboard.
	Instantly, the boat came to land,
	The place they were headed toward.
6:22	The crowd had seen the disciples
	Without Jesus leave the shore,
	And take the one and only boat.
	So Jesus they did look for.
6:23	The next day several boats arrived
	From Tiberias to the banks,
	Near the place where they had eaten
	After the Lord had given thanks.

6:24	When the crowd came to realize
	That Jesus was not around,
	They took the boats to Capernaum
6:25	Where Jesus they finally found.

"Rabbi, what time did You get here?"
To Jesus the crowd did say.
Jesus answered back with these words:
6:26   "Listen to this truth, I pray:[23]

"You seek Me not because of signs
But because you were filled with bread.
Don't work for food that perishes
But food that endures instead.

6:27   "The Son of Man will give you food.
Eternal life is the meal,
For God the Father placed on Him
His approving seal."

6:28   "What must we do to work God's works?"
They wanted to know what He meant.
6:29   "This is the work of God," He said,
"Believe in Him whom He sent."

6:30   "What miracle do You perform
That from You we can see
So that in You we may believe?
What miracle might this be?

6:31   "Our ancestors ate the manna
In the wilderness of doom.
The Scripture says, 'He gave them bread,
Out of heaven to consume.'"

The Poetic Scriptures of John

6:32   "Truly, truly, it's not Moses
Who from heaven gave you bread.
My Father gives you the true kind
That comes from heaven," He said.

6:33   "For the bread of God is this type,"
Jesus then defined.
"That which comes down out of heaven
And gives life to mankind."

6:34   "Lord, give us this bread every time!"
The crowd to Jesus pled.
Jesus responded back to them,
"I am the life-giving bread!

6:35   "The one who comes to Me in faith
Hungry he'll never be.
And neither will he ever thirst,
The one who believes in Me.

6:36   "But what about you who found Me?
You I've already addressed
That even though you have seen Me,
In Me your faith does not rest.

6:37   "All whom the Father gives to Me,
To Me in faith they'll come,
And he who comes to Me in faith,
I'll never cast out or shun.

6:38   "For I have come down from heaven
Not to accomplish My will,
But to do that of the Father
Who sent Me to fulfill.

6:39	"The Father's will for Me is this: That of those to Me He gave, I lose none, but on that last day I raise each from the grave.
6:40	"My Father's will is also this: For all who in Him believe, For all those who look to the Son, Eternal life they'll receive. "And I Myself will raise him up. (The believer is what I say.) I will raise him up from the grave On that very last day."
6:41	The Jews began to grumble much Because of this bold claim When Jesus said, "I am the bread, That down from heaven came."
6:42	They were saying to each other, "Isn't Jesus this Man's name? Isn't He the son of Joseph?" Objecting to His claim. "We know His father and mother. We know where He's really from. So how is it that He can say, 'Down from heaven I have come.'?"
6:43	Now while the Jews were conversing, Jesus answered them and said, "Stop the grumbling among yourselves." They were to listen instead.

6:44 "No one can come to Me unless
The Father draws him, I say.
I will raise him up from the grave
On that very last day.

6:45 "'And they all will be taught by God,'
In the prophets is what we read.
All who have heard and learned from God
In faith come to Me, indeed.

6:46 "No person has seen the Father,
No person but one, I mean.
He is the One who is from God.
The Father He has seen.

6:47 "Truly, truly, I say to you,"
Jesus went on and explained,
"The person who believes in Me
Eternal life he's obtained.

6:48 "I Myself am the living bread,
6:49 But manna your fathers ate.
They consumed it in the desert,
Yet death became their state.

6:50 "This is the bread which has come down,
Coming from heaven on high,
So anyone may eat of it
And never ever die.

6:51 "I am the living bread," He said,
"Who down from heaven came.
If anyone eats of this bread
He will forever remain.

        "And the bread is what I will give.
        This bread is My flesh, you see,
        And I will give it in exchange
        For the life of humanity."

6:52   The Jews argued with one another
        On the method of this feat.
        "So how can this Man give to us
        His flesh that we may eat?"

6:53   "You can't ever have life until
        The Son of Man's flesh you eat,
        And you must also drink His blood.
        This truth[24] I must repeat.*

6:54   "My flesh you must eat; My blood drink,"
        Jesus continued to say.
        "I will raise up all who do this,
        On that very last day.

6:55   "True food is My flesh, My body.
        My blood, the drink that's true.
6:56   Whoever consumes these abides
        In Me and I in him too.

6:57   "As the living Father sent Me
        And because of Him I live,
        So will also he who eats Me
        Since life to him I give.

6:58   "This is the bread which has come down,
        Coming from heaven's door,
        Not the kind our dead fathers ate.
        This gives life evermore."

The Poetic Scriptures of John

6:59   In Capernaum's synagogue
            Jesus was teaching this word.
6:60   Many of His disciples asked,
            After His words they heard:

            "These are very difficult words.
            Who is able to understand?"
6:61   And Jesus, knowing what they said,
            Gave them this reprimand:

            "Are My teachings too difficult?
            Do they cause you to stumble?
            What if you saw this with your eyes?
            Would you then still grumble?

6:62   "What if you saw the Son of Man,
            Going up to heaven on high,
            Going to where He was before?
            How would you then reply?

6:63   "It is the Spirit who gives life.
            No profit the flesh does receive.
            My words are spirit and are life,
6:64   But some of you don't believe."

            Jesus knew from the beginning
            Of those who did not believe.
            He also knew which one it was
            That would betray *and deceive.

6:65   "For this reason," Jesus explained,
            "I've said none can come to Me
            Unless this has been granted him,
            From the Father, you see."

6:66	At this time many disciples Withdrew and followed no more.
6:67	He asked the Twelve, "How about you? What would you want to leave for?"
6:68	Simon Peter replied to Him, "Lord, to whom would we go? You have words of eternal life, The only one we know.
6:69	"We believe and know who You are. You are God's Holy One. You are the Christ, the Messiah.[25] You are the Promised One."*
6:70	Jesus replied, "You are the Twelve. It is I who've chosen you! Yet one of you is a devil, And, yes, I know who."
6:71	Judas Iscariot, Simon's son, Was the person whom He meant. Although he was one of the Twelve, To betray Christ he'd consent.

7:1	Jesus avoided Judea Where the Jews wanted Him dead. So He continued traveling Throughout Galilee instead.

7:2	Now the Jewish Feast of the Booths Was coming very near.
7:3	His brothers, therefore, said to Him, "Why not depart from here?
	"To Judea why not return So Your disciples can see All the works that You are doing? Why not work openly?
7:4	"For no one does things secretly When he seeks to be known. Since You are doing all these works, To the world You must be shown."
7:5	Jesus's brothers said these things, Not out of courtesy,* But since in Him they did not trust, They spoke disrespectfully.*
7:6	Jesus replied, "It's not My time, But anytime you can go.
7:7	The world can't possibly hate you, But the world, it hates Me so.
	"The world hates Me for what I say. 'Their deeds are evil,' they hear.
7:8	So go up to the feast yourselves. My time is not yet near."
7:9	And having said these things to them, He stayed in Galilee.
7:10	Then after they went to the feast, He went up secretly.

7:11	The Jewish leaders sought Him out
	As they attended the feast.
	"Where is He?" they would ask each one.
7:12	About Him talk never ceased.
	Some were saying, "He's a good man."
	Others, "He leads them astray."
7:13	Yet none were talking openly,
	Fearing the leaders[26] that day.
7:14	This feast lasted for one full week,[27]
	And about halfway through,
	Into the temple Jesus went.
	To teach He began to do.
7:15	The religious leaders marveled,
	Conversing as He taught,
	"How has this Man become learned?
	Educated He is not!"
7:16	Jesus said, "The teachings aren't Mine,
	But are from Him who sent Me.
7:17	The one who wants to do His will,
	This that person would see.
	"For he'd be able to discern
	If from God My teachings came,
	Or if I speak from My own self,
	He surely could ascertain.
7:18	"The one who makes up what he says,
	His own glory that one seeks;
	But the one who seeks God's glory,
	The truth that person speaks.

"I seek the glory of the One
Who sent Me to address.
In Me there is only the truth,
And no unrighteousness.

7:19 "Did not Moses give you the Law,
Which none of you carry out?
Why are you plotting to kill Me?
This breaks the Law, no doubt."

7:20 "You must have a demon in You,"
The crowd replied with a shout.
"Who is it that seeks to kill You?
Whom are You talking about?"

7:21 "You all have marveled at one deed,"
To the crowd He did say,
"A miracle that I performed
Upon the Sabbath day.

7:22 "Moses gave you circumcision
From the ancestral way,
Commanding you to circumcise
On the Sabbath day.

7:23 "If to keep the Law of Moses
On the Sabbath you cut away,[28]
Why be angry because I healed
An entire man that day?

7:24 "Do not make impulsive judgments
Based on what you might see.
Stop judging Me by appearance,
But judge Me righteously."

7:25	Some people from Jerusalem
	Among one another said,
	"Is this the Man whose life they seek?
	Do not they want Him dead?
7:26	"Yet note that He speaks openly.
	Nothing to Him they say.
	Surely the rulers do not think
	He is the Christ, do they?
7:27	"But we do know about this Man.
	We know from where He's come,
	But whenever Christ does arrive,
	None will know where He's from."
7:28	"You both know Me and where I'm from!"
	In the temple Jesus cried,
	"I haven't come from My own will."
	He taught as He testified.
	"The One who sent Me, He is true.
	Him you don't know, that's clear,
7:29	But I do since I am from Him,
	The One who has sent Me here."
7:30	They were attempting to seize Him
	For saying where He was from,
	But no one laid a hand on Him.
	His time had not yet come.
7:31	But many there believed in Him.
	Others there just complained,
	"The Christ would do more miracles,
	Much more than what He's claimed."

7:32	When the Pharisees heard the crowd Muttering and not content, Joining along with the chief priests, For officers they sent.
7:33	"For a short time I'll be with you," Jesus went on to declare, "Then I'll go to Him who sent Me, A place you know not where.
7:34	"You will seek Me when I am gone, But Me you will not find, For where I am you cannot come."
7:35	These words confused their mind.*
	"Where does this Man intend to go, That Him we will not find? He is not intending to go To the scattered of our kind?
	"He is not intending to teach Among the Greeks, is He?
7:36	Just what does He mean by these words?" The Jews asked curiously.
	"What does He mean when He declared, 'You'll seek Me yet not find, For where I am you cannot come'?" These words confused their mind.*

7:37	Now on the last day of the feast,
	The greatest and highest day,
	He was standing before the crowd,
	Speaking in a loud way.

"If anyone among you thirsts,
Just come and drink from Me;
7:38 Whoever in Me does believe,
As Scripture does decree:

"'Out of his innermost being,
Rivers will continue to flow.
Yes, rivers of living water
Out of his belly will go.'"

7:39 He was speaking of the Spirit,
Whom those who in Him believe,
After He would be glorified,
As promised, would receive.

7:40 Some of the crowd began to say
As soon as they heard this quote,
"This certainly is the Prophet
About whom Moses wrote."

7:41 Others were saying, "He's the Christ."
Still others said, "It can't be!
Surely the Christ cannot arise
From Galilee, can He?

7:42	"Does not the Scripture clarify From David's line He'll come, Out of the town of Bethlehem, The village David was from?"
7:43	So there arose, because of Him, Division within the lot,
7:44	And some wanted to capture Him, But touch Him they did not.
7:45	So the officers came before The chief priests and Pharisees. Then the officers were questioned Why Him they did not seize.
7:46	"None ever speaks the way He does," The officers reported.
7:47	"Have you also been led astray?" The Pharisees retorted.
7:48	"Not one ruler or Pharisee Has ever in Him believed.
7:49	But this crowd, which knows not the Law, They're cursed for being deceived."
7:50	There was a ruler among them Who'd come to Jesus before, Who was known as Nicodemus. Their words he could not ignore.
7:51	"Our Law does not judge any man Unless it hears him first And knows the things he is doing," Nicodemus conversed.

7:52	They said, "Are you from Galilee? Through the Scriptures search and roam. No prophet comes from Galilee."
7:53	Then everyone went home.

8:1	But to a mountain Jesus went, Mount Olives, as it's known.
8:2	He then, early in the morning, Returned to the temple zone.
	And all the people came to Him. So He sat down as He taught,
8:3	But the scribes and the Pharisees, A woman they had brought.
	She was caught in adultery. They set her for all to see.
8:4	They said, "Teacher, this one's guilty. An adulteress is she.
8:5	"The Law of Moses commands us That such women we must stone, But what do You say?" they asked Him, "What action would You condone?"
8:6	To Jesus they posed this question So as to trap Him some way, Having some grounds to accuse Him In whatever He might say.

	But down to the ground Jesus stooped,
	And with His finger He wrote,
	Saying nothing, only writing.
	It was a silent note.*

8:7   Insisting that He answer them,
He stood and in a loud tone
Exclaimed, "You who are without sin,
Go ahead, throw the first stone!"

8:8   Again, He stooped down to the ground,
And began to write again,

8:9   And the people left one by one,
Starting with the oldest men.

Jesus, being the last one there,

8:10 Asked her as He arose,
"Is there no one to condemn you?
Where are they do you suppose?"

8:11 "There's no one, sir," she said to Him.
He said, "Be going along.
I do not condemn you either,
But no more live in wrong."

8:12 Jesus said to the Pharisees
In the temple that same day,
"I am the light of all mankind.
I will show them the way.

          "The one who keeps following Me,
          In darkness will never live.
          That one will have the light of life,
          The life which I will give."

8:13   The Pharisees then answered Him,
          "Of Yourself You testify.
          Your testimony can't be true.
          You must be speaking a lie."

8:14   Jesus answered and said to them,
          "Even if I testify,
          Bearing witness of My own self,
          It is true; it is no lie.

          "For I do know from where I came,
          And where I'm going to.
          Where I'm from and where I'm going,
          You don't have a clue.

8:15   "You all judge by fleshly standards,
          And this I do not do,
8:16   But even if I were to judge,
          My judgment would be true.

          "For I am not all by Myself.
          You judge Me by what you see.
          There is someone who's by My side,*
          The One who has sent Me.

8:17   "Even in your Law it's written
          The witness of two is true.
8:18   I bear witness of My own self.
          The Father who sent Me does too."

8:19 The Pharisees then questioned Him,
"Tell us where Your Father is?"
"You don't know Me nor my Father,"
Jesus answered their quiz.

"If you really knew about Me,
My Father you'd also know."
8:20 In the treasury He spoke these words,
Where the offerings would go.*

As Jesus taught in the temple,
Although no favor was won,
Nobody laid a hand on Him,
For His time had not yet come.

8:21 He said, "I am going away,
And to find Me you will try,
But you can't come where I'm going,
And in your sin you will die."

8:22 "He will not kill himself, will He?"
The Jews discussed to and fro,
"For He states that where He's going
We are not able to go."

8:23 Jesus replied, "You're from below
Where from above I have come.
You yourselves belong to this world,
But it's not this world I'm from.

8:24 "Therefore, I am saying to you,
You'll die in a sinful state,
For unless you trust that I Am,[29]
For you it will be too late."

8:25	Puzzled they asked Him "Who are You?"
	So these words He did convey,
	"What have I been speaking to you
	All along the way?
8:26	"There are many things I could speak
	And judge about all of you.
	What I speak to the world I've heard
	From My Sender who is true."
8:27	He was speaking of the Father,
	But they knew not whom He meant.
8:28	So He spoke more of the Father
	Who Him down to earth had sent.*
	"When you lift up the Son of Man,
	Then a few truths you will learn.
	You will know My identity,*
	That I Am,[30] you will discern.
	"You will realize that what I do,
	I do not do on My own.
	I speak what My Father taught Me.
8:29	He has not left Me alone.
	"He who has sent Me is with Me
	So that everything I do
	I always do to please just Him.
	This you will realize too."
8:30	As Jesus taught to them these things,
	In Him some had their faith rest.
8:31	The Jews who only believed[31] Him,
	These ones Jesus addressed.

	"You who really live in My word,
	You truly will learn from Me,
8:32	And you will come to know the truth,
	And the truth will set you free."

8:33	They said, "We're Abraham's offspring.
	Enslaved to no one are we.
	Tell us what You mean when You say
	That we will become set free?"

8:34	"Truly, truly, I say to you,"
	To them this truth He gave,
	"Everyone whose lifestyle is sin
	Is certainly its slave.

8:35	"The slave does not remain a part
	Of the household on and on.
	The one who does remain always
	Is not the slave, but the son.

8:36	"So if the Son will set you free,
	Then free you will be indeed.
8:37	I know you're Abraham's offspring,
	But you don't live like you're freed.*

	"For you are plotting to kill Me.
	You have no room for My word.
8:38	I speak what I've seen from My Father.
	From yours you do as you've heard."

8:39	"Our father, he is Abraham,"
	To Jesus they reacted;
	"If you are Abraham's children,
	Then you would act as he acted.

8:40	"But you are seeking to kill Me, A man who's told you what's true, The truth which I have heard from God. This Abraham did not do.
8:41	"You live like your father," He said. They said, *"Our birth is not flawed. We weren't born by fornication. We have one father; He's God."
8:42	He said, "If God were your Father, Me you certainly would love, For I Myself have come from God. I am here from above.
8:43	"For I did not come on My own. That One sent Me, it is clear; Why can't you understand My word? Because My word you can't hear.
8:44	"You all belong to your father, And want to do his bidding. Your father was a murderer From the very beginning.
	"And he does not stand in the truth Because in him there's none. Whenever he does speak a lie, From himself it does come.
	"For this is your father's nature: He is not on the level.* He's a liar and fathers them. Your father is the Devil.

8:45	"It is because I speak the truth,
	You do not believe in Me.
8:46	Who among you convicts Me of sin?
	Which one of you will it be?
	"Why are you not believing Me
	When I'm speaking what is true?
8:47	The one who does belong to God,
	His words he listens to.
	"The reason that you do not hear
	His words whenever I speak,
	Is because you do not belong
	To God whom you should seek."
8:48	The Jews answered and said to Him,
	"Have we not said it best
	That You are a Samaritan,
	And You are demon-possessed?"
8:49	"I have no demon," Jesus said,
	"A lie is what you decree.
	My Father is whom I honor,
	And you do not honor Me.
8:50	"My own glory I do not seek.
	The one Judge seeks it for Me;
8:51	If anyone obeys My word,
	Death he will never see."
8:52	"Now we know You have a demon,"
	To Him the Jews replied,
	"Abraham is dead, not just him,
	The prophets also died.

"Yet You say that if anyone
Obeys the word You teach,
Will never ever taste of death,
Which are bold claims to preach.

8:53 "Yes, Abraham, our father, died,
The prophets eventually.
Surely You're not any greater.
Whom are You claiming to be?"

8:54 "If I glorify self," He said,
"My glory would be flawed,
But Me My Father glorifies,
And you claim Him as your God.

8:55 "You have not known Him, but I do.
If this I were not to say,
I would be a liar like you,
But Him I know and obey.

8:56 "Your father Abraham rejoiced
At the hope of seeing My day,
And when he saw it, he was glad,"
All these things Jesus did say.

8:57 The Jews answered and said to Him,
"Just how long is Your life span?
You are not yet fifty years old,
And have You seen Abraham?"

8:58 Jesus replied, "I state the truth.
Prior to Abraham,
Before this man was even born,
I Am That I Am."[32]

8:59	They picked up stones to throw at Him.
	To kill Him was their intent,
	But Jesus merely hid Himself,
	And out of the temple went.

9:1	Jesus was walking by a man
	Who from his birth had been blind.
	When His disciples saw the man,
9:2	A question came to their mind.
	The disciples asked Him, "Rabbi,
	Just why was this man born blind,
	Because he sinned or his parents?
	The answer we want to find."*
9:3	Jesus answered, "Neither are right.
	It was not because of his sin
	Or due to that of his parents
	That his blindness he was born in.
	"But there's purpose for his blindness.
	It is for God to display
	His works within this man born blind
	Upon this very day.
9:4	"We have to work the works of God,
	Of Him who sent Me, I say.
	Night is coming when none can work.
	Let's work while it is still day.

9:5	"As long as I am in the world,
	I am its true light, I say.
	Night is coming when none can work.
	Let's work while it is still day."*
9:6	Saying this, He spat on the ground.
	He mixed the wet with the dry.
	He made some mud for the blind man,
	Smearing it upon each eye.
9:7	"Go and wash your eyes in that pool,
	Siloam," (the word means *sent*).
	The blind man obeyed, washed his eyes,
	And able to see he went.
9:8	Those who knew him as a beggar,
	Neighbors and passersby,
	Were saying, "Is this the blind man
	Who would for money cry?"
9:9	Some were saying, "That's the same man!"
	Others, "He's like him though."
	But each time the man would answer,
	"I am that beggar you know."
9:10	They asked the beggar to explain,
	"How are you able to see?"
9:11	He explained, "The Man called Jesus,
	A miracle did He.
	"He made some clay and rubbed my eyes.
	'To Siloam,' was His decree,
	'Go wash your eyes.' And this I did.
	Then I was able to see."

9:12   "Where is Jesus?" they asked the man.
       "I know not where to find."
9:13   So to the Pharisees they brought
       The man who had been blind.

9:14   When Jesus opened this man's eyes,
       Remember that He made clay.
       The Pharisees had Sabbath rules,[33]
       And it was the Sabbath day.

9:15   The Pharisees asked the beggar
       To explain how this could be.
       "On both my eyes He rubbed some clay.
       I washed them and now I see!"

9:16   "He's not from God," some of them said,
       "For the Sabbath Jesus breaks."
       Others asked, "How can a sinner
       Produce the signs that He makes?"

       There was division among them.
9:17   So they quizzed the man again,
       "Because this Man opened your eyes,
       What do you say about Him?"

       The man answered, "He's a prophet."
9:18   So then the Jews did decide
       That he was never blind before,
       That about his sight he lied.

       But then they called the man's parents
9:19   To question them thoroughly,
       "Is this your son you say was blind?
       How then did he come to see?"

9:20   His parents answered them and said,
       "We know him to be our son.
       We know, too, that he was born blind,
       And blindness he now has none.

9:21   "But how our son has come to see,
       We don't know; *that question's tough;
       We do not know who cured his eyes.
       Ask him! He is old enough!"

9:22   In this manner his parents spoke
       Because they were afraid,
       Because the council had declared
       This agreement they had made:

       "All who confess Jesus as Christ
       Will forever be thrown out,
       And barred from all the synagogues."
       This spread fear all about.

9:23   For this reason the parents said,
       "Ask him! He is old enough!"
       They had fear of being expelled.
       The penalty was too tough.*

9:24   A second time the Jews summoned
       The man who had been healed.
       "We know Jesus is a sinner.
       Glorify God!" they appealed.

9:25   "I do not know," the man answered,
       "If He's a sinner or not,
       But I do know that I was blind,
       And that sight to me He brought."

9:26	They questioned him, "What did He do To open up your blind eyes?"
9:27	"I've already said," the man replied, "But your hearing it defies.
	"Why do you wish to hear it twice? Do you wish to follow Him? Do you want to be disciples, By hearing it over again?"
9:28	The Pharisees insulted him For saying what he just said. "You're a disciple of Jesus. We follow Moses instead.
9:29	"For we know God spoke to Moses, But as for this one fellow, We do not know where He is from," The Pharisees did bellow.
9:30	The man answered and said to them, "Now me this does surprise. You do not know where He is from, Yet He opened my blind eyes.
9:31	"We know that God never listens To those who practice sin. The godly one who does His will, God does listen to him.
9:32	"No one has ever heard of one Healing one blind from birth.
9:33	If this Man did not come from God, He could do nothing of worth."

9:34   "You were born completely in sins,"
       The Pharisees did shout.
       "Do you think that you can teach us?"
       And then they threw him out.

9:35   Jesus heard that from the synagogue
       This person they did ban.
       Finding him, He asked this question,
       "Do you trust the Son of Man?"

9:36   The man replied, "Who is He, sir,
       That faith in Him I can place?"
9:37   Jesus said, "He is whom you've seen.
       He is talking to your face."

9:38   The man confessed, "Lord, I believe!"
       And fell down and worshipped Him.
9:39   Jesus said, "It's due to judgment
       That this world I've entered in.

       "I've come so those who cannot see,
       Their sight from Me can find,
       And those who think they really see
       May come to know they're blind."

9:40   Now some Pharisees were with Him,
       And with Him did not agree,
       "What are You saying about us?
       We are not blind, are we?"

9:41	"If you were blind, you'd have no sin," Jesus went on to explain, "But since you think that you can see, Your sin, it does remain.
10:1	"The one who does not use the gate To go into the sheep pen, But enters in some other way, Is a thief and robber then.
10:2	"I am speaking the truth to you. The person who goes inside, Using the gate to the sheep pen, Is the sheep's shepherd and guide.
10:3	"To him the doorkeeper opens, And his voice every sheep heeds. The shepherd calls his sheep by name, And those are the sheep he leads.
10:4	"When he brings out all of his sheep, Ahead of them he does go, And all of his sheep follow him Because his voice they know.
10:5	"They won't follow any stranger. From all strangers they will run Because they do not know the voice Of any stranger, not one."
10:6 **10:7**	Jesus used this figure of speech, But to them it was not plain What He meant by all of these words. So He went on to explain.

	"Again, I'm telling you the truth,
	The gate for the sheep am I.
10:8	All who came before Me are thieves.
	To them the sheep don't reply.

10:9	"I am the gate," Jesus explained,
	"All who enter through Me
	Will be saved, going in and out.
	Pasture they will always see.

10:10	"The thief comes just to do bad things:
	To steal, kill, and destroy.
	I came that the sheep might have life,
	Abundant life *filled with joy.

10:11	"I am the shepherd, the good kind,
	For the sheep My life I lose.
10:12	A hired hand is no shepherd.
	To die he would never choose.

	"A hired hand does not own sheep.
	So if the wolf were to come,
	He'd leave the sheep and flee the scene,
	The wolf snatching as sheep run.

10:13	"He'd flee since he's a hired hand.
	The sheep he does not mind.
10:14	I know My sheep and they know Me,
	The shepherd who's good and kind.

10:15	"This is like My Father and Me.
	Each other we really know.
	I know My sheep, and they know Me.
	For them My life I forgo.

The Poetic Scriptures of John

10:16 "I have sheep that aren't in this fold.
To bring them also I must.
They'll hear My voice; become one flock;
In one shepherd will they trust.

10:17 "This is why the Father loves Me,
Because I willingly die,
And I do this in such a way
That death's grip I defy.

10:18 "No one can take My life from Me,
But I lose it on My own.
I'm authorized to lay it down
Also death to dethrone.

"I have received this commandment
From My Father up above
To lose My life and take it back
For all the sheep that I love."

10:19 Due to these words that Jesus spoke,
The Jews disagreed again,
10:20 "He has a demon; He's insane.
Why do you listen to Him?"

10:21 But others said, *"That makes no sense,
Demon-possessed He can't be,
For a demon can't say such words,
Or heal the blind, can he?"

10:22	There took place in Jerusalem
	The Feast of the Dedication.
10:23	It was winter at the time
	Of this Jewish celebration.
	Jesus was walking in the place
	Called Solomon's portico,
	A sheltered part of the temple,
	A popular place to go.[34]
10:24	The Jews came around Him saying,
	"Do not keep us in the dark.
	So if You truly are the Christ,
	Give us a clear remark."
10:25	Jesus answered, "I have told you,
	Yet with faith you don't reply.
	The works I do in My Father's name,
	Of Me these testify.
10:26	"You don't believe for this reason,
	To My sheep you don't belong.
10:27	My sheep, whom I know, hear My voice,
	And behind Me follow along.
10:28	"I give eternal life to them,
	They'll never die, understand!
	No one has the ability
	To snatch them out of My hand.

10:29	"My Father gave the sheep to Me, And who is greater? There's none! No one can snatch them from His hand.
10:30	I and the Father are one."
10:31	The Jews took stones to throw at Him.
10:32	He said, "Much works I have shown. You've seen good works from the Father. For which will you throw a stone?"
10:33	"For a good work we don't stone You, But because of blasphemy. Because although You're just a man, God You claim to be."
10:34	Jesus answered, "Look in your Law, 'I said, you are gods' was spoken.
10:35	God's Word came to these He called gods. The Scripture cannot be broken.
10:36	"Now since the Father sanctified And into the world sent Me, Because I say, 'I am God's Son,' How is that blasphemy?
10:37	"If I don't do My Father's works, Then don't believe I'm true,
10:38	But if so, though Me you distrust, Believe the works I do. "Do this so that you may believe And come to really know That the Father, He is in Me, And I'm in Him also."

10:39	Again they tried to capture Him.
	He escaped and went away.
10:40	He traveled beyond the Jordan
	To a certain place to stay.
	It was where John had first started
10:41	His baptism ministry,
	And as Jesus was staying there,
	Many came to Him to see.
	They said, "While John performed no sign,
	Yet the truth he did declare.
	He spoke the truth about this Man."
10:42	Many believed in Him there.

11:1	In the village of Bethany
	Where Mary and Martha did stay,
	A certain man named Lazarus
	Became very sick one day.
11:2	Mary and Martha were sisters.
	(Mary was one who would care
	To pour perfume on the Lord's feet
	Then wipe them with her hair.)
	Now Lazarus was their brother.
11:3	So this message they did send:
	"Lord, come and see the one You love.
	He's ill, and he's Your friend."[35]

11:4	But Jesus said, when hearing this, "This is not so he will die, But this is to give God glory, And His Son to glorify."
11:5	Jesus loved Martha and Mary. He loved Lazarus so,
11:6	Yet when He heard that he was sick, For two days He did not go.
11:7	Then He said to His disciples, "Let's go to Judea again."
11:8	"Rabbi, the Jews tried to stone You. Why would You go near those men?"
11:9	Jesus answered and said to them, "Are not there twelve hours of light? One can safely walk in the day, Because the sun gives him sight.
11:10	"But surely a person will stumble If he walks in the night. He will stumble for this reason, Because in him there's no light."
11:11	After speaking this He then said, "Our friend has fallen asleep, But I'm going to wake him up. This promise I must keep."
11:12	"Lord," the disciples said to Him, "If he's sleeping, he'll awake!"
11:13	But Jesus meant Lazarus had died. His words they did mistake.

	They thought He meant literal sleep.
11:14	So Jesus plainly said,
	"Lazarus is not merely resting.
	Our friend is really dead!

11:15 "And I am glad I was not there,
For your sake, I mean to say,
In order that you may believe.
So let us go on our way."

11:16 Now to his fellow disciples,
Thomas, the Twin,[36] did sigh,
"Let us go to Judea too,
That with Jesus we may die."

11:17 When Jesus came near Bethany,
The burial already occurred.
Lazarus was lying in the tomb
For four days was the word.

11:18 From Jerusalem many Jews came,
About two miles away,
11:19 To comfort Martha and Mary
About their brother that day.

11:20 When the word had come to Martha
That Jesus was coming by,
While Mary stayed inside the home,
She went out to ask Him why.

11:21	"Lord, if You had been here on time,
	My brother would not have died,
11:22	But I still know that God will give
	Whatever You ask," she cried.
11:23	"Your brother," He said, "will rise again."
	She replied without question,
11:24	"I know he'll rise on the last day,
	In the resurrection."
11:25	"I'm the resurrection and life,"
	To her was His reply.
	"He who believes in Me will live,
	Even if he should die.
11:26	"And everyone who is alive
	And in Me their faith does cleave,
	These ones will never, ever die.
	Is this what you believe?"
11:27	She said, "Yes, Lord, I have believed
	That You are the Christ, God's Son.
	You are He who enters the world.
	You are the Promised One."*
11:28	Having said this, she went back home,
	And called her sister, Mary.
	She said, "The Teacher is calling you,"
	In a voice that did not carry.
11:29	Mary arose immediately,
	And was on her way to Him.
11:30	He was not in the village yet,
	But was where Martha had been.

11:31	The Jews who were comforting her Followed her, for they assumed, That she was going out to weep Where Lazarus was entombed.
11:32	When she came to where Jesus was, She fell at His feet and said, "Lord, if You would have come on time, My brother would not be dead."
11:33	When Jesus saw Mary weeping, And the Jews wailing their best,[37] In His spirit Jesus just groaned As He was greatly distressed.
11:34	"Where have you laid him?" Jesus asked. "Lord, come and see," they said;
11:35 **11:36**	When Jesus wept, they concluded, "He loved this man who's dead."
11:37	Some of them said, "Could not this One, Who healed the man born blind, Have healed this man from his sickness So death would not be assigned?"
11:38	Jesus, again groaning within, Went up to Lazarus's grave. Now there was a stone against it Because it was a cave.
11:39	He said to them, "Remove the stone." Martha objected and said, "Lord, by now there will be a stench. For four days he has been dead."

11:40	He told Martha, "Did I not say
	That if faith you would just own,
	You will see the glory of God?"
11:41	So then they removed the stone.

Then Jesus raised His eyes and said,
"Father, I thank You today
That Me You have already heard,
But out loud I now must pray.

11:42   "Even though You have heard My heart,
I say these words for this crowd.
So they will believe You sent Me,
I now am praying out loud."

11:43	After He said all of these things,
	Jesus loudly gave this shout:
	"Lazarus, come forth from the tomb!"
11:44	Then he who had died came out!

His hands and feet were restricted,
Being wrapped up in grave clothes.
Also his face was wrapped with cloth,
But from the tomb he arose.

Jesus then commanded the crowd,
"Untie him, and let him go."

11:45   Many Jews who came with Mary,
Saw and then trusted Him so.

11:46	Some of the others went away,
	Reporting what they had seen.
	Telling this to the Pharisees,
11:47	A council then did convene.

The chief priests and the Pharisees
Gathered together their minds.
"What are we to do about this,
For this Man does many signs?

11:48 "If we let Him continue this,
All will trust Him, each Jew!
Then the Romans will come and take
Our job and our nation too."

11:49 A certain man named Caiaphas,
Who was high priest that year,
He said, "You know nothing at all.
You all have too much fear!

11:50 "You can't see that it is better
That for all one man must die
So the whole nation won't perish."
11:51 This he did prophesy.

These words did not originate
From within his own mind.
Because he was high priest that year,
These words the Spirit assigned.

He also said that Jesus's death
Was for those scattered abroad,
11:52 That He would die to bring together
All of the children of God.

11:53 So they plotted from that day on
Just how Him they would kill.
Although He had done all these signs,
They plotted together still.

11:54	He stopped walking among these Jews So Him they could not view. Near the desert, to a city, To Ephraim He withdrew.
	He stayed there with His disciples Until the Passover was near.
11:55	When the Passover was at hand, Many Jews left from here.
	Jews went up to Jerusalem Before the Passover came To come and purify themselves
11:56	As they spoke of Jesus's name.
	"What do you think? Will Jesus come To the feast at all this week?" In the temple they would ask this While for Jesus they did seek.
11:57	The chief priests and the Pharisees Ordered reports to be sent By all who knew where Jesus was. To seize Him was their intent.

12:1	Six days before the Passover To Bethany He did head, To the place where Lazarus was, Whom He had raised from the dead.

12:2 They made Jesus a supper there,
And Martha served the food.
Some were reclining with Jesus.
Lazarus this did include.

12:3 Expensive perfume Mary took,
From a spikenard plant it came,
And poured from a twelve-ounce[38] vial
On Jesus's feet without shame.

She wiped the feet she anointed
By using her own hair.
The aroma from the perfume
Completely filled the air.

12:4 But then Judas Iscariot,
A disciple of the Lord,
Who intended to betray Him,
Objected to what she poured.

12:5 "Now why was not this perfume sold
And given to the poor?
Three hundred days' wages[39] it's worth.
It's gone and is no more!"

12:6 Now the reason why he said this
Was not from care for the poor.
It was because he was a thief.
Money he did adore.

He was the one who was in charge
Of the treasury purse.
He would take money for himself,
And did not reimburse.

12:7	Jesus replied, "Leave her alone.
	It's for My burial day.
	She has kept it for that reason."
	He continued on to say:
12:8	"People living in poverty
	Will always be around,
	But that is not the case with Me.
	She did not waste the pound."*
12:9	A large number of Jews had learned
	Where Jesus had been staying.
	As soon as they had heard the news,
	They came without delaying.
	Not only just to see Jesus,
	To this place they had sped,
	They wanted to see Lazarus
	Whom He raised from the dead.
12:10	The chief priests planned Lazarus's death
12:11	Since many Jews were leaving,
	For on account of Lazarus,
	In Jesus they were believing.
12:12	On the next day the crowd of Jews,
	Who to the feast had come,
	Heard that toward Jerusalem
	Jesus's journey had begun.
12:13	They took the branches from palm trees,
	And went out to meet the Lord.
	"Bless Him who comes in the Lord's name,"
	They shouted in one accord.

	"Hosanna! He's King of Israel!"
	They cried out in one voice.
12:14	Jesus found a little donkey
	And sat on it by choice.
	For a prophecy is written,
12:15	"Zion's daughter do not fear.
	Look! Seated on a donkey's colt,
	Your king is coming near."
12:16	His disciples did not discern
	That of Him it was prophesied
	Until these things they remembered
	After Jesus was glorified.
12:17	The crowd that testified of Him
	Was the same one at the cave
	When He had raised up Lazarus,
	Calling him out of the grave.
12:18	For this reason another crowd
	Went out to Jesus to meet,
	Because they heard He had performed
	This miraculous feat.
12:19	The Pharisees were conversing,
	"Our plans just bring frustration.
	Look who is going after Him,
	The entire population."

The Poetic Scriptures of John

12:20   There were certain Greeks among them
          Who were going to the feast
          For the purpose of worshipping.
          Their paganism had ceased.[40]

12:21   They met Philip from Bethsaida,
          Which is in Galilee.
          They asked him, "Sir, will you tell us?
          Jesus we wish to see."

12:22   Philip relayed this to Andrew,
          And to Jesus they both went,
          Telling Him of the Greeks' desire
          That for Him they had sent.

12:23   Jesus answered, saying to them,
          "The hour has now arrived.
          Time has come for the Son of Man
          To be glorified.

12:24   "Truly unless a grain of wheat
          Falls into the earth and dies,
          It remains as a single seed,
          But in death much grain will rise.

12:25   "The person who loves his own life,
          His life he will destroy,
          But he who hates it in this world,
          Eternal life he'll enjoy.

12:26	"All who serve Me continually Must keep following Me So that whatever place I'm at There My servant will be.
	"If anyone keeps serving Me, He'll be honored by the Father.
12:27	Because My soul is now troubled, With this plea should I bother:
	"'Father, save Me from this hour!"? This hour is why I came. No, but this is what I will pray,
12:28	'Father, glorify Your name!'"
	A voice from heaven spoke these words After Jesus spoke His cry, "I have both glorified My name, And My name I'll glorify."
12:29	When the nearby crowd heard the voice, Some said that thunder was heard. Others were saying that the voice Was an angel speaking a word.
12:30	Jesus answered and said to them, "This voice has spoken out loud Not because I had to hear it. It spoke for this very crowd.
12:31	"It's now time for judgment to come Upon this very world. It is now time for its ruler Out of heaven to be hurled.[41]

12:32	"Since from earth I'll be lifted up,
	To Me I'll draw all men nigh."
12:33	Jesus said this to indicate
	The kind of death He would die.

12:34	They said, "Christ will live forever.
	This from the Law we've heard.
	So how can He, the Son of Man,
	Be lifted up? That's absurd!

"Tell us, who is this Son of Man?"
An answer they did incite.
12:35 Jesus, therefore, replied to them
With words of darkness and light.*

"For just a little while longer
Among you the light will shine.
So that darkness won't consume you,
Walk in this light of Mine.

"The one who walks in the darkness,
Where he walks he can't perceive.
12:36 While you have the light before you,
In the light you must believe.

"That way you may be sons of light."
He spoke these words out loud,
And from them He then departed,
And hid Himself from the crowd.

12:37 Although He had done many signs
Before them to be eyed,
They still did not believe in Him.
12:38 This Isaiah prophesied:

"Who has believed our report, Lord?
To whom has His arm been shown?"
This prophecy they did fulfill
With their unbelieving tone.*

12:39 This is why they could not believe:
Since Isaiah also said,
12:40 "The Lord has blinded both their eyes,
And their heart He has made dead.

"So with their eyes they cannot see,
Or with their heart perceive,
So they can't repent and be healed."
That's why they could not believe.

12:41 Isaiah spoke these very things
Since His glory he observed
In a vision given to him.
About Jesus was his word.

12:42 Yet many among the rulers,
In Jesus their faith did rest,
But because of the Pharisees,
This they had not confessed.

12:43 They feared that from the synagogue
They would be cast out then,
For instead of God's approval,
They loved the favor of men.

12:44 "The one who does believe in Me
Does not trust in Me alone,
But also in the one true God
Who sent Me, His very own."

12:45 Jesus continued crying out,
"The one who looks at Me
Views more than what he's looking at.
My Sender he does see.

12:46 "I have entered the world as light
So all who believe in Me
Would not remain in the darkness,
But in Me they could see.

12:47 "If anyone hears My sayings,
Yet them he does not mind,
I Myself will not judge that one,
For I've come to save mankind.

12:48 "He who rejects Me and My words
Now has a judge, I say.
The word I spoke will be his judge
On that very last day.

12:49 "For the words I speak are not Mine.
The Father's words I convey.
He who sent Me gives the command
What to speak and to say.

12:50 "His command holds eternal life.
Therefore, the things I say,
I speak just as He has told Me,
Not any other way."

13:1   Before the Feast of Passover,
Jesus knew the time had come
For Him to go out of this world
To the Father where He's from.

He loved all those who were His own,
His disciples whom He chose,*
Disciples whom were in the world.
He loved them to the close.

13:2   There was Judas Iscariot,
Simon Iscariot's son,
Celebrating the Passover,
Thinking what had to be done.

By this time Satan, the Devil,
Had planted in his heart
To betray the Lord Jesus Christ
Before the meal did start.

13:3   Jesus knew the Father had placed
All things into His command,
And that He had come forth from God,
And would return as planned.

13:4   So during the meal He got up.
His garments He laid aside.
He took a towel, wrapping it.
Around His waist He tied.

13:5	He poured water in a basin. Then His disciples He faced. Jesus washed their feet and wiped them With the towel from His waist.
13:6	When He came to Simon Peter, To Jesus, Peter said, "Lord, will You be washing my feet?" There was a sense of dread.*
13:7	Jesus answered and said to him, "You now don't realize why. After I'm done washing your feet, Then you'll identify."
13:8	"Wash my feet, You will never do!" He wouldn't let Him start. Jesus said, "If I don't wash them, With Me you have no part."
13:9	"Then Lord, I ask, not just my feet," To Him Simon Peter said, "I ask that You wash more than that, My hands, also my head."
13:10	Jesus replied, "All who have bathed, Their body cleaning is done. All they need is to wash their feet. You all are clean except one!"
13:11	The reason why He had said this Was because He did mean That Judas would soon betray Him. Judas was not clean.

13:12	Jesus put His garments back on After washing their feet; "Do you know what I have just done?" He asked as He took His seat.
13:13	"You are right in what you call Me, Calling Me Teacher and Lord.
13:14	Since I washed each one of your feet, This task you should afford.
13:15	"For I have set an example For washing one another's feet.
13:16	Listen to these parallel truths,[42] So this command you may meet.
	"A slave in no way surpasses The master on whom he waits, Nor is a messenger above The one who to him dictates.
13:17	"Since you well know these things are true, You will surely be blessed If you wash one another's feet As I have already stressed.*
13:18	"I do not speak to all of you. My chosen ones I know, But very soon will be fulfilled This Scripture from long ago.
	"David has written in the Psalms Of a friend who shared a meal,[43] 'The one who eats my bread with me Has betrayed me with his heel.'

13:19	"At this time I am telling you, Before it comes to plan, So that when it does come to pass, You may believe that I Am.[44]
13:20	"He who receives those whom I send, Receives Me. The truth I tell, And the one who does receive Me Receives My Sender as well."
13:21	After Jesus had said all this, His spirit became distressed. "I tell the truth that one of you Will betray Me," He addressed.
13:22	The disciples began to stare. One another they did survey. They had no clue which one of them That Jesus said would betray.
13:23	The disciple whom Jesus loved Was reclining by His chest.
13:24	So Simon Peter gestured him His identity to request.
13:25	So leaning back on Jesus's chest, "Who is it, Lord?" he muttered.
13:26	"The one to whom I give dipped bread, He's the one," Jesus uttered.
	When Jesus dipped a piece of bread, He put it in Judas's hand, The son of Simon Iscariot. Then He gave a command.

13:27	For after Judas took the bread,
	Into Judas, Satan went.
	So Jesus said, "What you have planned,
	Quickly implement."

13:28 Those reclining did not realize
Why Jesus gave this command.
13:29 Some had supposed it was because
He had their money in hand.

Some thought he was supposed to buy
For the Feast of Unleavened Bread,[45]
Or that he was supposed to give
So the poor could be fed.

13:30 As soon as Judas took the bread,
He departed right away,
And it was night time when he left.
13:31 Then Jesus began to say:

"The Son of Man is glorified,
And God, too, in the Son.
13:32 Since in Him God is glorified,
This event will be done:

"God will glorify in Himself
The Son immediately.
13:33 Little children, I am with you.
For a short time it will be.

"You will seek Me, and as I said
To the Jews some time ago,
'Where I'm going, you cannot come.'
I say that to you also.

13:34	"A new command I give to you That you love one another. In the same way I have loved you, You, too, love every brother.
13:35	"In this practice all men will know That you're disciples of Mine: If each of you toward the other Unselfish love does shine."
13:36	Simon Peter said to Jesus, "Where, Lord, will You have gone?" "Where that is, you cannot come now, But you'll follow later on."
13:37	Peter replied, "Lord, tell me why I can't follow You right now? For You I will lay down my life. Why won't this You allow?"
13:38	"Will you lay down your life for Me?" To Peter, Jesus replied. "Truly a cock won't crow before Me you have thrice denied."

14:1	Jesus then turned to the others, "Don't let your heart be distressed. Since you all place your faith in God, Also in Me let it rest.

14:2	"For in the home of My Father Are many places to live. If there were no dwelling places, Other instruction I'd give.
14:3	"I am going for this reason, To prepare a place for you, And since I'm leaving to do this, I will surely return too. "And when I do come back again, I'll take you to be with Me So that whatever place I'm at There you may also be.
14:4	"And the place to where I'm going, You know the way," Jesus taught.
14:5	Thomas barked, "Lord, how can we know? Where You're going we know not!"
14:6	Jesus replied, "I am the way. I'm the truth and the life too. No one can come to the Father Unless Me they come through.
14:7	"If you've really come to know Me, My Father you'd also know. From now on you really know Him, And Him you have seen also."
14:8	Philip said, "Lord, show the Father. For us that's all we need."
14:9	"Philip, I've been with you this long, Yet Me you know not indeed.

"He who sees Me has seen Him too.
'Show us the Father,' you call?
14:10 I am in Him, and He's in Me.
Don't you believe this at all?

"The words that I am telling you,
From Me they do not come.
The Father who in Me abides
Does His works in His Son.

14:11 "Believe that I'm in the Father.
The Father is in Me too.
At least believe the works themselves,
The works you see that I do.

14:12 "Truly, truly I say to you,
He who in Me believes,
He will do the works which I do,
Even greater works than these.

"He will do greater works than these
Since to the Father I go,
14:13 And all that you ask in My name,
That will I do also.

"This way the Father in the Son
May be glorified.
14:14 So all you ask Me in My name,
The work I will provide.

14:15 "If you love[46] Me unselfishly,
My commandments you will live,
14:16 And from the Father I will ask.
Another Helper He'll give.

	"When the Father gives the Helper,
	He'll forever be with you.
14:17	This One is the Spirit of truth.
	Receive Him, the world can't do.

"The world can't receive this Spirit
Since Him they don't know or see.
Since He is with you, you know Him,
And inside you He will be.

14:18 "I will not leave you as orphans,
But I'll come back to your place.
14:19 Soon the world will see Me no more,
But you will behold My face.

"Because I live, you too will live.
14:20 In that day you will construe
That I'm in the Father, you're in Me,
And I am in you too.

14:21 "He who receives My commandments,
And them he keeps obeying,
He's the one who really loves Me,
Unselfishly, I am saying.

"The one who loves Me in this way,
My Father's love he will know.
I will love him unselfishly,
And Myself to him I'll show."

14:22 Judas (but not Iscariot),
This question he then hurled,
"Lord, why would You disclose Yourself
To us but not the world?"

14:23 "If anyone really loves Me,"
Jesus answered back,
"That one will keep heeding My word.
God's love he will not lack.

"My Father and I will come to him.
Our home with him We'll make.
14:24 He who does not truly love Me,
My words he does forsake.

"The teaching which you hear from Me,
To Me does not belong,
But the Father who has sent Me,
It's come from Him all along.

14:25 "I have spoken these things to you
While I am with you abiding.
14:26 The Helper, the Holy Spirit,
Will in you be residing.

"In My name the Father will send
The Spirit to teach everything.
All that I have spoken to you,
To your memory He will bring.

14:27 "I'm leaving peace behind with you.
It is My peace that I give,
Not the peace that the world offers.
In My peace you will live.

"So don't let your heart be distressed,
Or let it be filled with fear.
14:28 I've told you that I'm going away,
But to you I'll reappear.

         "If you've loved Me unselfishly,
         Joy would be your heart cry
         Because I go to the Father,
         For He is greater than I.

14:29   "At this time I have told you this
         Before it comes about,
         So that when it does come to pass
         You'll believe without a doubt.

14:30   "I will not speak much more with you,
         For there is coming the hour
         When comes the ruler of this world.
         In Me he has no power.

14:31   "As the Father commands, I do,
         That the world may come to know
         That I really love the Father.
         Arise! From here let us go.

15:1   "My Father is the gardener.
         The true vine I portray.
15:2   Each branch in Me that bears no fruit,
         That branch He cuts away.

         "But every branch that does bear fruit
         He prunes so it bears more.
15:3   However, you are pruned[47] at last
         By the word I spoke before.

15:4   "Abide in Me. I'll be in you.
Alone a branch can't bear.
It has to abide in the vine.
So abide in Me, I declare.

15:5   "I am the vine; you're the branches.
If in Me one does abide,
Much fruit will be produced by him,
For in him I reside.

"There is nothing that you can do
That is apart from Me.
15:6   All who do not in Me abide,
Like a useless branch he'll be.

"Useless branches are thrown away,
And enter a withering phase.
They are gathered for the fire
And then are set ablaze.

15:7   "If you keep abiding in Me
And My words in you abide,
You can ask whatever you wish,
And it shall be satisfied.

15:8   "This is to My Father's glory
That abundant fruit you bear,
Proving to be My disciples
By your actions you declare.*

15:9   "Just as the Father has loved Me,
That way I've loved you too.
This love is sacrificial love.
Reside in My love for you.

15:10	"If you obey My commandments, In My love you will reside, Like I keep My Father's commands And in His love abide.
15:11	"These things I have spoken to you," Jesus went on to teach, "So that My joy may be in you, And fullness it might reach.
15:12	"This commandment I give to you That this kind of love you show, Unselfish love to one another. I've loved you this way, you know.
15:13	"Greater love has no one than this, When a person pays the price, Laying his life down for his friends, The ultimate sacrifice.
15:14 **15:15**	"If you do what I command you, You truly are My friends. No longer will I call you slaves. That relation it transcends. "For a slave does not ever know All that his master might do, But I have called you all My friends. So I share all this with you. "All that I've heard from My Father, To you I did disclose.
15:16	Not one of you has chosen Me, But all of you I chose.

"I have appointed all of you
To bear fruit that will remain
That My Father will give to you
All you ask in My name.

15:17 "My command is love one another,
15:18 But if the world hates you,
Realize that it hated Me first.
Don't be shocked when they do.*

15:19 "If you all belonged to this world,
The world would love you then,
But I chose you out of the world.
So the world hates you, men.

15:20 "Remember when I washed your feet
These words that I had stated,
'A slave in no way surpasses
His master on whom he's waited.'

"If the world persecuted Me,
They'll persecute you someday.
If the world has obeyed My word,
Your word they will obey.

15:21 "But these things they will do to you
For My name's sake, you see,
Because they do not really know
The One who has sent Me.

15:22 "If I had not spoken to them,
They would not have any guilt,
But since I have spoken to them,
No excuses can be built.

15:24	"If I had not done among them Works which no others had done, They would not be guilty of sin, But their guilt has now begun.
15:23	"He who hates Me hates My Father. Me they have seen and hated. So they hate My Father as well, As I've already stated.*
15:25	"Now their hatred fulfills these words Found in this Scripture clause (Remember that it's in their Law), 'They hated Me without cause.'
15:26	"One day I will send the Helper. From the Father He will come. The Helper is the Spirit of truth. The Father He is from.
	"When the Helper comes down to you, Of Me He will testify.
15:27	Since you've been with Me from the start, Testimonies you'll supply.

16:1	"These things I have spoken to you So that you'll not go astray.
16:2	They'll bar you from the synagogues, And you they will cast away.

"The time will come for all to think,
Who target you and kill,
That to God they'll be offering
A service to His will.

16:3 "And all of these things they will do
Since they have never known
The Father who is in heaven
Or Me, though Him I've shown.[48]

16:4 "So these things I am telling you
That when their time arrives,
You'll remember what I have said
Of those who want your lives.

"I did not say these things to you
From the very start
Because I was still with you all.
It was not time to depart.*

16:5 "The time for Me is very near
To go up to My Sender,
Yet you don't ask Me where I'll go.
This question you don't render.

16:6 "Now since I've said these things to you,
Sorrow has filled your heart,
16:7 But truly it is for your good
That from this world I part.

"For the Helper can't come to you
If on this earth I stay.
So I will send Him down to you
Since I am going away.

16:8	"When He comes He'll convict the world About this very thing, Sin and righteousness and judgment, And why conviction bring?
16:9	"He will convict concerning sin Since Me they do not trust.
16:10	He will convict of righteousness Since go from here I must.
	"After I go to the Father, Me you'll no longer behold.
16:11	The Helper will convict the world Of judgment that will unfold.
	"Because the ruler of this world, Condemned he already stands, The Helper will convict the world Of the judgment God demands.
16:12	"I have much more to say to you, But this you now can't bear.
16:13	When He comes, the Spirit of truth, He will guide you with care.
	"Into all truth He will guide you, For He won't speak on His own, But what He hears He'll speak to you. What's to come He'll make known.
16:14	"Me the Spirit will glorify Because from Me He will take, And what that is He'll show to you. He will do this for My sake.

16:15 "Everything that the Father owns,
These belong to Me too.
That's why I said, 'From Me He'll take,
And will show it unto you.'

16:16 "In just a little while from now
You'll see me no more then,
Yet a little while after that
My face you'll see again."

16:17 Some of Jesus's disciples
Between them began to confer,
Seeking the meaning of His words.
But questions that's all they were.*

"What does He mean by telling us,
'You'll see me no more then,
Yet a little while after that
My face you'll see again'?

"What does He mean by this reason,
'Because to the Father I go?'
16:18 What's He mean by 'a little while?'
His meaning we do not know."

16:19 Now Jesus knew it was their wish
To ask Him what He meant.
So He began to question them,
And here is how that went:

"Are you discussing what this means:
'You'll see me no more then,
Yet a little while after that
My face you'll see again'?

16:20	"The truth[49] is that you will lament. While the world is glad, you'll mourn. In very deep grief you will be, Yet to joy it will transform.
16:21	"A woman in labor has pain Since it's time to birth whom she bore, But when she gives birth to her child, She recalls the pain no more.
	"For her joy surpasses her pain Because of the child she's borne. As the child comes into this world, To joy her pain does transform.
16:22	"Likewise you now are filled with pain, But soon you'll see My face. Then your heart will greatly rejoice With a joy none can erase.
16:23	"Now in that day you see My face With joy you'll be overcome, And you won't ask Me anything, No questions, not even one.
	"Truly, truly, I say to you, If to the Father you cry, Requesting from Him anything, In My name He will supply.
16:24	"You've not yet asked for anything In My name, did you know? Keep on asking, and you'll receive That your joy may overflow.

16:25	"I have spoken these things to you By using figures of speech. The time is near when this I'll stop. Of the Father I'll plainly teach.
16:26	"In that day you'll ask in My name. But this I am not saying That I ask God concerning you, That I just do the praying.
16:27	"For the Father loves[50] you dearly Since Me you deeply love,[51] And since you also have believed I've come from Him above.
16:28	"From the Father I have come forth, And into the world of men I'm returning to the Father. I'm leaving, I say again."
16:29	His disciples responded back, "We're listening to You teach. Now You're speaking very plainly Without figures of speech.
16:30	"So now we know You know all things. Our inquiries You don't need. By this we trust You are from God: Our hearts You know indeed."
16:31	Jesus answered and said to them, "You are believing at last,[52]
16:32	But behold a time is coming That soon will be the past.

	"You'll be scattered, each to his home,
	And Me alone you will leave,
	And yet alone I will not be.
	To Me the Father will cleave.
16:33	"I speak that you'll have peace in Me.
	In the world you will have none.
	Tribulation is what you will have,
	But don't fear. I've overcome."

17:1	After Jesus said all these things,
	To heaven He fixed His gaze,
	"It's time to glorify Your Son
	That the Son may give You praise.
17:2	"For, Father, You have given Him
	Power over men who live
	So that to all You've given Him
	Eternal life He may give.
17:3	"And this describes eternal life:
	A personal faith is meant,
	To really know[53] the one true God
	And Jesus Christ whom You've sent.
17:4	"You I glorified on this earth
	Through the work You had Me do.
	I've finished the work and mission.
17:5	Now glorify Me with You.

"Father glorify Me with You
With the glory I had in hand.
Restore the glory I possessed
Before the world did stand.

17:6   "The men You gave Me from this world,
To them Your name I've conveyed.
They were Yours whom You gave to Me,
And Your word they have obeyed.

17:7   "They have now come to the knowledge
That everything I possess
Comes from You, which You gave to Me,
Even all that I express.

17:8   "For the words You have given Me,
To them I have imparted.
They know I'm from You and You sent Me.
Now their faith has started.

17:9   "So I'm asking on their behalf.
For the world I do not plea,
But for those who belong to You
Which You have given Me.

17:10 "And all that I possess is Yours,
And all that's Yours is Mine.
And in them I've been glorified
Both in this world and time.

17:11 "When I am no more in the world,
In the world they will remain.
Since I will be coming to You,
Protect them in Your name.

"Holy Father, protect them all
With Your name You gave Your Son
That they may all be unified
As You and I are one.

17:12 "I was keeping them in Your name,
The name You've given Me.
While I was with them I did this:
I guarded them carefully.

"And I have lost not one of them
According to what You willed
Except the son of destruction
So that Scripture be fulfilled.

17:13 "But I'll be coming to You now.
So in this world I address
That, overflowing within them,
My joy they may possess.

17:14 "I have given to them Your word,
But them the world abhorred,
For to the world they don't belong
As I don't; *I'm their Lord.

17:15 "But to take them out of this world,
No, this I am not pleading,
But I'm asking that You keep them
From the evil one's *leading.

17:16 "Like Me, they are not of this world.
17:17 In the truth sanctify them.
Set them apart from this world.*
Your word is truth. Amen.[54]

17:18	"I have sent them into the world
	Just as You have sent Me.
17:19	I sanctify Myself for them
	That sanctified they may be.

	"So sanctify them in Your truth,
17:20	But for just them I don't pray.
	I also pray for those who trust Me
	Through the word they convey.

17:21	"As You're in Me, and I'm in You,
	Unite them, Father, as one
	That the world may trust You sent Me.
	Unite them in You and Your Son.

17:22	"The glory which You've given Me,
	To them I have supplied
	That they may also be as one
	Like We are unified.

17:23	"You are in Me, and I'm in them.
	So perfect them in unity
	That the world may know I was sent
	And You loved them as You loved Me.

17:24	"Father, I want these You gave Me
	To be with Me where I am,
	To see My glory I shared with You
	Before the world began.

	"For before all time You loved Me,
17:25	And righteous Father, these know
	That You sent Me, and I know You,
	Though the world hated You so.

17:26	"I have made known Your name to them, And will continue to do That the love which You loved Me with May with Me be in them too."

18:1	After Jesus had prayed these words, With His disciples He passed Beyond the Valley of Kidron And into the garden at last.
18:2	Now Judas knew about this place (Judas who would betray), For Jesus often brought them there, And would withdraw *to pray.
18:3	This Judas brought Roman soldiers And officers to accuse, The officers from the chief priests And the Pharisees of the Jews. Now Judas was leading this band Into the garden at night. They came with weapons and torches And lanterns to give them light.
18:4	Jesus knew about all these things. These things the Father did speak.* He went to meet this band and asked, "Whom is it that you seek?"

18:5	They answered Him, "We seek Jesus, Jesus the Nazarene." Judas, who was betraying Him, Was with them at the scene.
18:6	Jesus replied to them "I Am."[55] These words they did astound. The band of men stepped back in shock And fell right to the ground.
18:7	Jesus questioned them once again, "Whom is it that you seek?" They said, "Jesus the Nazarene." These words He then did speak:
18:8	"I told you My identity. I Am, these words receive. If, therefore, you are seeking Me, Let My disciples leave."
18:9	Jesus guarded His disciples, And His words were fulfilled, "Of all those whom You've given Me, I've lost none as You willed."
18:10	Simon Peter, having a sword, Drew it, having no fear, And struck Malchus, the high priest's slave, Severing his right ear.
18:11	Jesus ordered Simon Peter, "Return your sword to your side! Can't I drink from My Father's cup That to Me He did provide?"

18:12   The commander and the soldiers
             And officers of the Jews
             Arrested Jesus and bound Him
             As soon as they heard this news.

18:13   They led Jesus to Annas first,
             A man they did revere,
             The father-in-law of Caiaphas
             Who was high priest that year.

18:14   (Caiaphas had advised the Jews
             It was better for one to die
             In place of the Jewish nation.
             This he did prophesy.)

18:15   Now with another disciple
             Peter did follow behind
             And came to the high priest's courtyard
             With a doorkeeper assigned.

             The *other* was the high priest's friend.
             So he entered in the yard
             Along with Jesus and the mob,
             But Peter, he was barred.

18:16   As Peter stood outside the door,
             The *other* did decide
             To speak words to the doorkeeper
             Who then let Peter inside.

18:17   The doorkeeper was a slave girl.
             To Peter she did say,
             "Are not you that Man's disciple?"
             To which he said, "No way!"

18:18 Now the slaves and the officers
Were cold just standing there.
Therefore, they made a charcoal fire
To keep warm in that air.

Now Peter was also with them,
And he was also cold.
He warmed himself over the fire
As the questioning did unfold.

18:19 The high priest confronted Jesus
With many questions that night,
Concerning all His disciples
And His doctrinal insight.

18:20 "I've taught the world in open places,"
Jesus began to state,
"In synagogues and the temple
Where Jews congregate.

"There's nothing I spoke in secret.
18:21 So why do you question Me?
Ask the hearers what I taught them.
They know, I guarantee."

18:22 An officer, standing nearby,
Struck Jesus with a blow.
"This is not the way to answer,
A high priest, don't You know?"

18:23 "If I've spoken incorrectly,
Point out the wrong I said,
But if I have spoken rightly,
Why strike Me in the head?"

18:24	So Annas sent Jesus away,
	Since no answers could be found,
	To the high priest Caiaphas,
	And Jesus they kept bound.
18:25	Simon Peter was standing near,
	Keeping warm by the fire.
	"Aren't you one of His disciples?"
	The officers did inquire.
	Peter replied, "No! I am not!"
	Jesus he did deny,
18:26	But the one whose ear Peter chopped
	Had a relative nearby.
	He also was the high priest's slave,
	And Peter he did indict,
	"Did I not see you with this Man
	In the garden this very night?"
18:27	Peter again denied his Lord
	Whom he really did know.
	As soon as he denied the Lord,
	He heard a rooster crow.

18:28	Jesus was led from Caiaphas
	Into Pilate's headquarters,
	But since the dawn had not yet come,
	The Jews stopped at its borders.

They did not want to be defiled
By entering a Gentile's place,*
But wished to eat the Passover.
So they entered not this space.

18:29 So Pilate went out to the Jews,
For a charge had not been brought.
"What accusation do you bring
Against this Man I've got?"

18:30 The Jews answered and said to him,
Being defensive this time,*
"We would not have brought Him to you
If He committed no crime!"

18:31 Pilate replied, "Take Him yourselves.
By your law judge this Man."
The Jews said, "But we're not allowed
To put to death as you can."

18:32 This fulfilled the word of Jesus
When He did prophesy
To the crowd that had heard God's voice[56]
The kind of death He'd die.

18:33 Pilate returned to his palace
Since death they could not choose.
He summoned Jesus and asked Him,
"Are You the King of the Jews?"

18:34 Jesus replied, "Why do you ask?
Is this from your own thought?
Or do you ask because you've heard
Reports that others brought?"

18:35 Pilate answered, "I'm not a Jew
As You can plainly see.
Your own people and the chief priests
Delivered You up to Me!

"They brought You here for a purpose.
So tell me what You've done
To warrant such action by them,
Why their disfavor You've won."

18:36 "My kingdom is not of this world,"
Jesus began to reply.
"If My kingdom were of this world,
My servants would not stand by.

"No, My servants would be fighting
To keep Me from the Jews.
My kingdom is not of this realm
Since capture I did not refuse."

18:37 Pilate said, "So, You are a king?"
"You're correct," was His reply.
"I was born and entered this world
Of the truth to testify.

"All those who belong to the truth
Will listen to My voice."
18:38 But Pilate answered, "What is truth?"
To listen was not his choice.*

He went out again to the Jews,
"I find no criminal here,
18:39 But I'll release someone for you
As you demand each year.

"This is a Passover custom
That for you I will fulfill.
So whom should I release to you,
The King of the Jews? I will!"

18:40 But loud and clear the Jews cried out,
"He must not be acquitted,
But release to us Barabbas."
(Robbery he committed.)

19:1 But Pilate ordered Jesus scourged.
The soldiers did as he said.
19:2 They also wove a crown of thorns
And shoved it on His head.

They dressed Him in a purple robe
19:3 As Him they did disgrace.
"Hail, King of the Jews!" they would say,
Giving blows to His face.

19:4 Pilate went out before the Jews,
"Look! I'm bringing Him out.
I want you all to really know
He's innocent, no doubt."

19:5 Jesus came out before the crowd
With the crown upon His head,
Wearing also the purple robe.
"Behold, the Man!" Pilate said.

19:6 The chief priests and the officers
Shouted with a mighty cry.
Upon seeing Jesus they yelled,
"Crucify, Crucify!"

           But Pilate said, "Take Him yourselves.
           Crucify Him whom you've bound,
           But as for me I can't do this.
           No guilt in Him I've found."

19:7   The Jews answered, "We have a law,
           And by that law He must die,
           For He has claimed to be God's Son.
           That's why we yell, 'Crucify!'"

19:8   Now when Pilate heard this statement,
           His fear increased even more.
19:9   He went back into the palace
           With more questions to explore.

           He had Jesus brought before him.
           He asked "Where are You from?"
           But Jesus did not answer him,
           But stood before him dumb.

19:10   Pilate did not like His silence.
           "You do not speak to Me?
           Don't You know I have the power
           To crucify and set free?"

19:11   "You'd have no power over Me
           If from God it had not been.
           So he who gave Me up to you,
           He has the greater sin."

19:12   So Pilate tried to release Him.
           Protest the Jews did send,
           "If you release this Man we've brought,
           You are not Caesar's friend.

"For this Man makes Himself a king.
This claim is very well known,
And everyone who claims kinghood
Opposes Caesar of Rome."

19:13 When Pilate heard the words they said,
He brought Jesus outside
And sat down on the judgment seat,
Not wanting Him crucified.

The judgment seat was at a place,
The Pavement as it was known
(In Hebrew it's called *Gabbatha*),
Paved with all kinds of stone.[57]

19:14 It was the preparation day
For the Passover week.
Approximately six o'clock,[58]
"Behold, your king!" he did speak.

19:15 "Away with Him! Away with Him!"
The crowd began to chant.
"Crucify Him! Crucify Him!"
This Pilate would not grant.

"Am I to crucify your king?"
Sarcasm he did not lack.*
"We have no king except Caesar!"
The chief priests answered back.

19:16 Pilate finally gave in to them.
Their demands he could not deny.
He delivered Jesus over
For them to crucify.

19:17	They took Jesus, and He went out.
	His own cross He was to bear
	To the point called, "Place of the skull,"
	With two criminals there.
	In Hebrew it's called Golgotha,
19:18	And there they crucified,
	Not just Him, but two other men,
	Each one on either side.
	Jesus was in between the two,
19:19	And on His cross could be seen
	An inscription that Pilate wrote,
	"Jesus the Nazarene."
	After His name the crime was carved.
	"King of the Jews," it read.
19:20	In Hebrew, Latin, and in Greek,
	It was written overhead.[59]
	The place where He was crucified
	Was just outside the city.
	So many Jews read what was carved.
	On Jesus some had pity.*
19:21	Now the chief priests said to Pilate,
	"Why do you write this thing?
	Do not write 'The King of the Jews,'
	But that He claimed to be king."

19:22	"What I've written, I have written,"
	Pilate brought this to a close.
19:23	When the soldiers raised Jesus up,
	They divided up His clothes.

They tore the outer clothes in four,
Each soldier taking one,
But the tunic, it was seamless,
As one piece it was spun.

19:24	A soldier said, "Let's not tear it,
	But decide whose it will be
	By casting lots for this tunic."
	To this all did agree.

This fulfilled the words of Scripture,
Concerning David's foes,[60]
"My outer garments they did tear.
They cast lots for my clothes."

19:25	His mother, Mary, and her sister
	Were standing nearby the scene
	With Mary, the wife of Clopas,
	And Mary Magdalene.
19:26	Jesus looked and saw His mother
	Standing nearby the cross
	And the disciple whom He loved.
	They were feeling a great loss.*

He said to her, "There is your son!"

19:27	To him, "Your mother, behold!"
	This disciple from that time on
	Took her into his household.

19:28	Sometime later, Jesus knowing That all was done as God willed, Began saying, "I am thirsty," That Scripture might be fulfilled.
19:29	A jar full of sour wine was there. A sponge they then had dipped And put it on a hyssop branch To reach His mouth, which sipped.
19:30	"It is finished!" Jesus shouted. He had drunk the Father's cup,[61] And so He then bowed down His head. His spirit He gave up.

19:31	Now since it was a special day, The day of preparation, Anyone staying on the cross Would be a desecration.
	For the next day was the Sabbath, But a special one of those. The Jews wanted bodies removed Before this day would close.
	So they went and asked of Pilate If the deaths he could speed By breaking the legs of the men,
19:32	And the soldiers did this deed.

	They broke the legs of the first man,
	Then the man on the other side,
19:33	But when they examined Jesus,
	He had already died.

	Jesus's legs they did not break,
19:34	But a soldier pierced His side
	With the spear that was in his hand
	To make sure that He had died.

	Water and blood poured out of Him.
19:35	He who saw this testifies.
	He knows it is true; so believe,
	For what he speaks aren't lies.

19:36	Now this fulfilled the Scripture words,
	"No bone of His will break,"
19:37	And "They will look on whom they pierced."
	His life no man could take.*

19:38	Joseph of Arimathea,
	A burial he did choose.
	He was a secret disciple
	Because he feared the Jews.

	He asked Pilate for the body,
	And Pilate said, "All right."
19:39	Along with him was Nicodemus
	Who talked to Jesus one night.[62]

	About one hundred Roman pounds
	Of spices did he bring,
	A lavish mix of aloes and myrrh
	For Jesus Christ, the King.*

19:40	As was the custom of the Jews,
	With linen strips they wound
	Which held the mixture of spices
	Until He was fully bound.
19:41	Now at that place was a garden
	Where He was crucified,
	And in the garden a new tomb
	Which had not been occupied.
19:42	Because it was the Jewish day,
	The day of preparation,
	They laid His body in that tomb
	To avoid desecration.

20:1	Now on the first day of the week
	While it was still early and dark,
	To the tomb where Jesus was laid,
	Mary Magdalene did embark.
	When she had come up to the tomb,
	She saw the stone displaced.
	It was rolled up from the entrance.
20:2	So she ran from there in haste.
	When she came to Simon Peter,
	With him was another man
	(The disciple whom Jesus loved).
	To explain she then began.

"They have taken away the Lord
From the tomb," she conveyed,
"And we don't even have a clue
Where Him they might have laid."

20:3 So Peter and the other one,
To the tomb they did proceed.
20:4 Starting off they ran together.
Then the *other* took the lead.

That disciple came to the tomb
Before Peter had drawn near.
20:5 He saw the grave clothes lying there
As he began to stoop and peer.

He entered not into the tomb,
But stood there by the cave.
20:6 Then Simon Peter entered first
To analyze the grave.

The linen clothes were lying there
In the grave made of stone.
20:7 He saw the facecloth of the Lord
Rolled up in a place alone.

20:8 The other one then came inside.
He looked and then believed,
20:9 But the meaning of a Scripture
They had not yet perceived.

The Scripture was about the Christ,
That He must rise again.
20:10 Because they did not understand,
To their homes went these men.

The Poetic Gospel of John

20:11 Mary was weeping by the tomb.
         She stooped and looked while crying.
20:12 She saw two angels sitting there
         Where Jesus had been lying.

         They were sitting on either end
         Where Jesus's body was laid,
         One at the head, one at the feet.
         In white they were arrayed.

20:13 They said, "Woman, why do you weep?"
         She said, "For my Lord, I despair.
         They took His body somewhere else,
         But I do not know where."

20:14 When she said this, she turned around.
         She saw Jesus standing there,
         But as to His identity
         She was unaware.

20:15 He said, "Woman, why do you weep?
         Whom is it that you seek?"
         Thinking He was the gardener,
         She then began to speak.

         She said to Him, "Please tell me, sir,
         If You've carried Him away.
         Tell me where You have laid my Lord,
         And I will take Him today."

20:16 As Mary turned to walk away,
         She heard a familiar tone.
         "Mary," He spoke her very name.
         To her He made Himself known.

	She turned around and said to Him,
	"Rabboni," in her tongue.
	Translated this word means *teacher*.
20:17	To Jesus she just clung.

"Stop holding Me," He said to her,
"For there is much work to do.
I've not gone up to the Father,
And here is My work for you.

"Go report to all My brethren
That I'm going to ascend
To My Father who is My God,
On whom I do depend.*

"My Father, He is also yours.
He's My God and yours too.
Go report to all My brethren.
This is My mission for you."

20:18 Mary Magdalene went to tell.
To the disciples she did head.
"I have seen the Lord," she exclaimed,
And told them the things He said.

20:19 Now it was evening on that day,
The first day of the week.
The disciples were in hiding.
Their future had seemed bleak.*

            They had the doors shut very tight
            Out of fear of the Jews.
            Then Jesus appeared in their midst,
            And He gave them this good news.

            "Peace is with you!" Jesus exclaimed,
20:20 Showing His hands and His side.
            The disciples were overjoyed,
            Seeing their Lord who had died.

20:21 Jesus again exclaimed to them,
            "Peace with you!" was His shout,
            "Just as the Father has sent Me,
            So you I am sending out."

20:22 And after He had said these words,
            On them His breath He blew.
            "You receive the Holy Spirit,
            And these things you can do:

20:23 "If you forgive anyone's sins,
            Forgiveness will have been done.
            If you retain anyone's sins,
            Forgiveness there will be none."

20:24 Now Thomas, who was of the Twelve,
            Didymus was his nickname,
            He was not with them at this time.
20:25 So to him they did explain.

            They said to him, "We've seen the Lord!"
            But this he did not receive,
            "Unless I actually see the Lord,
            I will in no way believe!

"I must see the marks of the nails
From when He was crucified.
I have to put my finger there,
And my hand into His side."

20:26 Eight days later in that same place,
With the doors being shut tight,
Jesus appeared again to them.
Thomas was there for this sight.

"Peace is with you!" He said to them.
20:27 Then to Thomas He did command,
"Put your finger into the marks
Where the nails were in each hand.

"Now take your hand and put it here,
Where the spear had pierced My side.
No longer say you won't believe,
But believe I'm He who died!"

20:28 "O Jesus, my Lord and my God,"
Thomas exclaimed with delight.
20:29 Jesus said, "Since you have seen Me,
Your belief matches your sight.

"But many will come to believe,
Based on what others record.
Blessed are they that have not seen,
Yet believed I'm God and Lord."[63]

20:30 Jesus performed many more signs
Which are not written here.
He did them for His disciples
Whenever He did appear.

20:31 But the things written in this book
Are so that you may believe
That Jesus is the Christ, God's Son,
And life in His name you'll receive.

21:1 Sometime later Jesus appeared
To some disciples again
At the Sea of Tiberias,
Showing Himself to these men.

21:2 Simon Peter was one of them,
With Thomas called the Twin,
Also Nathanael from Cana.
(Galilee this town was in.)

There were four more along with them:
The sons of Zebedee,
And then two other disciples,
Making seven near the sea.*

21:3 Simon Peter announced to them,
"I am going out to fish."
They said to him, "We'll come with you."
To do this was their wish.*

They all got in a boat to fish,
And they rowed out from the shore.
They fished that night catching nothing.
Their wish had become a chore.*

21:4	Now when the day began to break,
	Jesus stood on the beach.
	They did not know that it was Him,
21:5	But they listened to His speech.
	"Children," Jesus called out to them,
	"You have no fish, do you?"
	They answered Him, "We have not one."
21:6	Then He told them what to do.
	"Cast the net on the boat's right side,
	And you will find a catch."
	They cast their net and it was filled
	With an amazing batch.
	So full was the net that they cast,
	They could not haul it on board.
21:7	The disciple whom Jesus loved
	Told Peter, "It is the Lord!"
	Simon Peter was stripped for work
	When receiving this word with glee.
	He then put on his outer clothes
	And dove into the sea.
21:8	They were one hundred yards away,
	Not very far from the sand.
	The others took the little boat,
	Dragging the fish to the land.
21:9	When they got out upon the land,
	They saw a charcoal fire
	With fish placed on it, also bread.
21:10	Then this He did require.

	"Bring of the fish you have now caught."
21:11	So Peter went out to haul,
	Drawing the net full of large fish,
	One hundred fifty-three in all.

He hauled the net onto the land,
And although it was packed,
The net was not torn anywhere.
The net was kept intact.

21:12   Jesus then said, "Come, have breakfast."
To question Him, all ignored.
They feared asking Him who He was,
But they knew He was the Lord.

21:13   Then Jesus came and took the bread,
And He passed it all around.
Likewise He gave to them the fish.
No questions did they sound.

21:14   This was Jesus's third appearance,
After rising from the dead,
That He made to His disciples,
And they ate some fish and bread.

21:15   Jesus said to Simon Peter
After they ate this meal,
"Simon, son of John, please tell Me
That your love is real.

"Do you love[64] Me unselfishly
More than you love these men?[65]
Do you love Me unselfishly
More than the fish hauled in?"

Peter replied, "Yes, Lord, I do.
My heart You know, You've read.
You know that I am friends with You."
"Feed My lambs," Jesus said.

21:16 A second question Jesus asked,
But with nothing to compare,[66]
"Do you love Me unselfishly?
Simon of John, now declare."

Peter replied, "Yes, Lord, I do,
My heart You know, You've read.
You know that I am friends with You."
"Care for My sheep," Jesus said.

21:17 A third question Jesus then asked,
"Simon, are you My friend?"[67]
He was so hurt by this third one
That grief through him it did send.

"You know all things. You know my heart.
Lord, You know I am Your friend."
To him Jesus gave the reply,
"My sheep you then must tend.

21:18 "Truly, truly, I say to you,
When you were just a lad,
You dressed yourself and walked around
According to the wish you had.

"When you become an older man,
You will stretch out your hands,
And others will put clothes on you
And lead you by their demands.

	"They will lead you against your will."
21:19	Jesus gave this prophecy
	That by death he'd glorify God.
	Then Jesus said, "Follow Me!"

21:20 As he began to follow Christ,
He turned around to see
The disciple whom Jesus loved,
Following eagerly.

(This is he who also leaned back
At that meal on Jesus's breast
And asked Him who would betray Him.)
21:21 Peter this question pressed.

"Lord, what's to happen to this man?"
21:22 Jesus to him did explain,
"What if I wished that he not die,
But on this earth remain?

"What if I wish that he not die,
But My coming he should see?
What does this have to do with you?
You just keep following Me!"

21:23 This word went out to the others,
"This disciple will not die,"
But that is not what Jesus meant.
This He did not imply.*

He was only making the point*
That Peter was to obey
No matter if that one would live
To see that final day.

21:24   The disciple whom Jesus loved
            Testified of what he knew
            And wrote these things down in this book,
            And we know his word is true.

21:25   Now Jesus did many more things,
            Which if written, I presume,
            All the space of the world itself
            For these books would have no room.

THE POETIC LETTERS OF JOHN

FIRST JOHN

1:1 That which was from the beginning,
Which we've seen with our eyes,
Which we've heard with our very ears,
Which we did analyze—

That which was from the beginning,
Which we handled with our hands—
We're referring to the Word of life
Manifested by God's plans.

1:2 The life was manifested here.
We proclaim what we've beheld,
Eternal life who was with the Father
And with Him always dwelled.[68]

1:3 We tell you what we've seen and heard
So your fellowship may be won.
Our fellowship is with the Father
And with Jesus Christ, His Son.

1:4   We are writing all of these things
So that our joy may be filled,
Up to the top, overflowing,*
And continuing to build.*

1:5   The message which we've heard from Him
To you we now declare,
That God is light, and within Him
There's no darkness anywhere.

1:6   If we claim fellowship with Him
Yet walk in darkness instead,
We lie and don't practice the truth.
We are spiritually dead.*

1:7   But if in the light we're thriving
As He is in the light,
These things are a reality*
About us in God's sight:*

       We fellowship with one another,
With each and every one.*
All our sin is cleansed by the blood
Of Jesus His only Son.

1:8   If we claim we no longer have sin,
Ourselves we are deceiving.
The truth is not really in us.
The truth we aren't receiving.*

1:9   If we keep confessing our sins,
He's faithful and just, no less,
To forgive our sins and cleanse us
From all unrighteousness.

1:10	If we claim we have never sinned, That no wrong we have incurred,* We make God to be a liar, And in us is not His word.

2:1	My little children, this I write That to sin you won't submit, But if one does happen to sin, We have an advocate. He's Jesus Christ the Righteous One Who before the Father's face[69] Keeps any charge from being brought By standing in our place.
2:2	He is the payment for all our sins. God's wrath on us can't fall.[70] The payment isn't for us alone; It's for the whole world, for all.
2:3	And we know we've truly known God If this test our life withstands,* If we truly have a lifestyle Of obeying His commands.
2:4	The one who says, "I've known Him," lies If in this he persists, In disobeying His commands. In him no truth exists.

2:5	But whoever lives the lifestyle
	Of obedience to His word,
	God's love has been perfected in him.
	God's love he has preferred.*

	By this we know that we're in Him,
2:6	If our life matches our talk.*
	He who says, "I abide in Him,"
	As Jesus lived he must walk.

2:7	Beloved, I'm not writing you
	A new commandment or word,
	But an old one you've had from the start,
	The message you have heard.

2:8	But in Christ's words[71] I'm writing you
	A commandment that is new.
	The truth of this is seen in Him,
	And that truth is seen in you.

        The old one is the new command
        That to us Christ did assign,[72]
        For the darkness is passing away
        As the true light now does shine.

2:9	The one who says he's in the light,
	Yet hatred describes his will,
	Hating him who is his brother,
	He's in the darkness still.

2:10	He who has the lifestyle of love
	Toward those who are his brothers,
	Abides in the light, and he's not
	A stumbling block to others.

2:11	He who has the lifestyle of hate (His brother he does despise) Walks in darkness, not knowing where Since darkness blinds his eyes.
2:12	Little children, I'm writing you To make this very plain:* Your sins have been forgiven you On account of His name.
2:13	And fathers, I am writing you Because you've really known Him who existed from the start; Your relationship has grown.* And youngsters, I am writing you Because you've overcome. You have conquered *Satan himself, Known as the evil one. Dear children, I have written you Because of whom you know; You're connected to the Father And intimately[73] so.
2:14	And fathers, I have written you Because of whom you know, Him who existed from the start, In whom you spiritually grow.* And youngsters, I have written you Since strength you have pursued; God's word abides inside of you, And Satan[74] you have subdued.

The Poetic Scriptures of John

2:15 Don't persist in loving the world
Or the things that are within,
For anyone who loves like this,
God's love is not in him.

2:16 For all that is within the world
The Father does not provide:
Lust of the flesh, lust of the eyes,
And life's arrogance and pride.

2:17 These things are from a passing world.
With its lusts it will be gone,
But he who practices God's will
Abides on and on.

2:18 Children, the last hour is here,
And this is how we know:
You've heard Antichrist is coming—
We've seen many come and go.

2:19 These antichrists are not of us,
But from us they went away
Because if they had been of us,
With us they surely would stay.

So they separated from us
In order for it to be shown
That they aren't really part of us;
Their action made that known.*

2:20   I do not need to tell you this*
Since all of this you know.
The anointing from the Holy One
Teaches you this also.

2:21   I write not because you don't know.
That's not the reason why.
I write because you know the truth
And since the truth can't lie.

2:22   Now tell me who is the liar?
It is the one who denies
The truth that Jesus is the Christ.
The truth can't teach such lies.*

Tell me who is the antichrist?
It's the one who denies
The truth of the Father and the Son;
The truth can't teach such lies.*

2:23   He who keeps denying the Son,
The Father he can't possess;
But he really has the Father
If the Son he does confess.

2:24   Let what you have heard from the start
Keep abiding in you.
Then you'll keep abiding in the Son
And in the Father too.

2:25   This is the promise that's for us
Which He Himself has made:
Eternal life He gives to us
Who in the Son has stayed.*

2:26	The things which I am writing you Is due to those who try To lead you into believing That which is a lie.
2:27	The anointing you received from Him In you continues to stay, And you've no need for anyone To teach you anyway.
	His anointing keeps teaching you All the things you've been taught. Since it is true and not a lie, Abide in Him as you ought.
2:28	Little children, abide in Him So that when He does appear, We may be truly confident And not shrink away in fear.
2:29	Since you know that He is righteous, This you know to be true, That all who practice righteousness, From Him have been born *anew.

3:1	The Father's love given to us, See how immense it is, That we are called children of God. Yes, we truly are His.

3:2	Dear ones, we now are God's children, But it has not been revealed What we'll be in eternity. This knowledge has been concealed.* But we know what we will be like When He appears in the sky. When we see the Lord as He is, We'll be like Him whom we eye.
3:3	Everyone who does hope in Him Purifies himself for sure, For when we fix our hope on Him, We're pure as He is pure.
3:4	He who has the lifestyle of sin Lawlessness he does pursue. Lawlessness is the lifestyle of sin, For sin is lawlessness too.
3:5	You know the reason He appeared. He came for sins to remove. In Him there is no sin at all. Of sin He does not approve.*
3:6	None that truly abide in Him Have the lifestyle of sin. Anyone who has this lifestyle Has never seen or known Him.
3:7	Let none deceive you, little ones,[75] You who are really His,* He who has a righteous lifestyle Is righteous as He is.

3:8	He who has a sinful lifestyle, To the Devil he belongs; For Satan has sinned from the start, Inspiring all kinds of wrongs.*
	The Son of God, He did appear, Having this purpose in mind, To destroy the works of the Devil, Sinfulness to unbind.*
3:9	The one who has been born from God Can't have the lifestyle of sin. He cannot since he's born from God Whose seed abides in him.
3:10	God's children and the Devil's, too, By their lifestyle are known. One can't be from God and not do right, And not love God's very own.
3:11	For from the very beginning, This message you have heard: We must keep loving[76] one another Unselfishly; that's His word.
3:12	Don't be like him who killed Abel. To the Devil belonged Cain. His deeds were evil; his brother's right. That's why his brother was slain.
3:13	My brothers, when the world hates you, Do not be shocked thereof.
3:14	We know we've passed from death to life Because our brothers we love.

He who has not a life of love,
In death he does abide.
Since he has a lifestyle of hate,*
He's empty of life inside.*

3:15   He who keeps hating his brother
Is also murdering him.
You know a murderer cannot have
Eternal life within.

3:16   We've experienced selfless love
When our Lord paid the price,
Laying His life down in our place,
The ultimate sacrifice.*

Because the Lord did this for us,
An example He does make.
So we ought to lay down our lives
For our brothers' sake.

3:17   He who has material things
But locks out feelings to give,
Seeing his brother in dire need,
How can God's love in him live?

3:18   Let us not love with word or tongue.
Little children, please obey.
Let us all love in deed and truth
By living the words we say.*

3:19   By deeds of love we truly know
That to the truth we belong.
Before Him it assures our heart
That condemns us in our wrong.

3:20	It assures us since God's greater
	Than our hearts and knows all things,
3:21	And if our heart condemns us not,
	Before God confidence rings.

3:22	Whatever we keep praying for,
	From Him we do obtain,
	For we keep His commands and do
	What's pleasing to His name.

3:23	His command is that we believe
	In the name of Christ,[77] His Son,
	And selflessly love one another
	As He commanded each one.

3:24	He who obeys His commandments,
	In Him he truly abides.
	He who has this lifestyle of faith,
	In him God truly resides.

In this way we truly realize
That in us God resides,
By His Spirit He's given us,
Whose Spirit in us abides.

4:1	Dear ones, don't trust every spirit,
	But each one you must test.
	See if they are really from God
	Before in their words you rest.

        Since many false prophets have gone out
        Into the world to preach,
        Test each spirit before you trust
        Everything they teach.

4:2   God's Spirit you experience[78]
        When truth is being taught.*
        This test apply so you can see*
        If it's from God or not:*

        Each one confessing Jesus Christ
        As One who in the flesh came,
        That spirit truly is from God,
        Attesting to His name.*

4:3   Each one not confessing Jesus
        As One who in the flesh came,
        That spirit cannot come from God,
        Not attesting to His name.*

        That's the spirit of antichrist,
        Of which you've heard will come.
        This spirit is now in the world,
        Denying Jesus, God's Son.*

4:4   Little children, you belong to God.
        These spirits you've overcome,
        For greater is He who's in you
        Than he *called the evil one.

        The evil one* is in the world,
4:5   To which false prophets belong,
        And so they speak as from the world,
        And the world does heed their wrong.

4:6　　He who knows[79] God personally
　　　　Will listen to what we say
　　　　Since we truly belong to God
　　　　And since the truth we convey.*

　　　　He who does not listen to us,
　　　　To God he does not belong.
　　　　That's how we know the spirit of truth
　　　　And the spirit of wrong.

4:7　　Let's love one another selflessly,
　　　　For love comes from God above.
　　　　All who know God, who are born from Him,
　　　　Pursue this lifestyle of love.

4:8　　He who does not have this lifestyle
　　　　That comes from God above,*
　　　　That one can't know God personally,
　　　　For God Himself is love.

4:9　　God's selfless love was shown to us
　　　　When time came for Him to give.
　　　　He sent His one Son into the world
　　　　That through Him we could live.

4:10　　This is love, not that we loved God
　　　　(The honor to God belongs)*
　　　　But that He loved us and sent His Son
　　　　As payment for our wrongs.

4:11　　Dear ones, since God loved us this way,
　　　　Then love we must pursue.
　　　　We too ought to love one another
　　　　By the deeds that we do.*

4:12   No one has seen God any time,
        But if love is our bent
        (Loving one another selflessly),
        Then God becomes evident.*

        If we really love one another,
        In us God truly abides.
        His love has been fulfilled in us.
        The unseen God resides.*

4:13   We truly know this abiding,
        God in us and us in Him,
        By the Spirit He's given us,
        The Spirit who dwells within.*

4:14   We have observed and testify
        Of what the Father has done.
        He's sent the Savior of the world,
        His one and only Son.*

4:15   If you confess Him as God's Son,
        In you God truly does dwell.
        Anyone who confesses this
        Abides in God as well.

4:16   We have experienced[80] God's love
        Which to us He did give.
        We have also trusted His love,
        And in His love we live.

        If your lifestyle is one of love,
        In God you truly dwell.
        God is characterized by love,
        And God is in you as well.

4:17	That's how love is fulfilled with us
	So boldness we will display.
	Since we are like Him in this world,
	We need not fear judgment day.
	There will be a day of judgment,
4:18	But in love there is no fright,
	For perfected love throws out fear,
	Wanting to be in His sight.*
	In the person fearing judgment,
	No love for God appears.*
	He has not been perfected in love
	Since punishment he fears.
4:19	The reason why we love at all
	Is due to this one fact:
	God came to us and loved us first
	So in love we then do act.*
4:20	If anyone says, "I love God,"
	Yet a life of hate does emit,
	Despising his Christian brother,
	That one is a hypocrite.
	Those without a loving lifestyle,
	Hating his brother in view,
	Can't love God whom he's never seen;
	No, this he cannot do.
4:21	He who truly has love for God
	Must love his brother too,
	Which commandment we have from Him.
	So love we must pursue.

5:1	All who trust Jesus as the Christ, By God have been born *anew, And whoever loves the Father Would love His child too.
5:2	The life of loving God's children We realize in this way: When we unselfishly love God And His commandments obey.
5:3	For this is selfless love for God: That His commands we obey. Since His commands aren't burdensome, Delight in living His way.*
5:4	For whatever is born of God Over the world does win; This is the victor over the world: Our faith that is within.
5:5	Who is it that conquers the world, But the one who does believe That Jesus is the Son of God, Whom that person did receive?*
5:6	Jesus Christ came by water and blood, Not in the water alone, In the water and in the blood, In which He made Himself known.*

5:7	It is the Spirit who testifies
	Because the Spirit is true.
5:8	The Spirit's witness does agree
	With the other two.

        For there are three that testify,
        And they are in harmony—
        The Spirit, the water, and the blood.
        Their witness does agree.

5:9   We accept the witness of men,
        Yet God's witness is greater.
        God has testified of His Son.
        So listen to the Creator.*

5:10 He who trusts in the Son of God
        Has the witness within.
        He who trusts not what God has said
        Is charging God with sin.

        When one doesn't trust God's witness,
        He is saying that God lies
        Since he has not trusted God's Son,
        Of whom God testifies.

5:11 This is the record of God's witness:
        Eternal life He's conferred;
        This life is received in His Son.
        That's the witness of His word.*

5:12 He who receives the Son has life,
        Eternal life, as I've said.
        He who does not receive God's Son,
        Has no life *but is dead.

5:13 I have written these things to you
Who in God's Son's name believed
So you may know that eternal life
You have truly received.

5:14 When we pray we can be assured
That to us He listens, still,
If we keep on petitioning Him
According to His will.

5:15 If we know He's listening to us
In whatever we might pray,
We know He's granted the request
Which on Him we did lay.

5:16 If anyone sees his brother
Persisting in a sin
(The kind that does not lead to death),
He must pray for him.

Yes, he must pray for his brother
Who is steeped in a sin.
In addition to constant prayer,
He must give life to him.

There is a sin that leads to death,
And if you see such a case,
I'm not saying you should ask God
To give that brother grace.[81]

5:17	Every unrighteous act is sin,
	No matter what it may be.*
	But there is sin that won't bring death.
	Pray when that kind you see.
5:18	We know those born of God can't have
	A lifestyle of sin as such.
	He who was born of God keeps him,
	And him Satan can't touch.
5:19	We know *that we are born of God,
	That to Him we do belong.
	We know the world's in Satan's[82] hands
	Under the power of wrong.*
5:20	We know God's Son has come and gives
	Understanding to us too
	So that we can experience[83] Him
	Who is genuine and true.
	We are in the One who is true,
	In Jesus Christ, His Son.
	He's the true God and eternal life.
5:21	So idols you must shun.

SECOND JOHN

1:1   The elder to the chosen lady
         And to her children too,
         Whom I selflessly love in truth
         As also these others do.

         All those who really know the truth
         Love you unselfishly
1:2   Because the truth abides in us
         And with us will always be.

1:3   With us will be grace, mercy, and peace
         From God the Father above,
         From Christ Jesus, the Father's Son,
         His Son in truth and love.

1:4   I became overwhelmed with joy
         When your children I saw
         Living in truth which we've received
         From the Father as law.

1:5   And now, lady, I'm writing to ask
         Not about anything new,
         But the same command which we've had,
         That we love one another too.

1:6	This is love: to pattern our lives After the commands He gave. This you've heard from the beginning: That by them you must behave.
1:7	For many have gone into the world— Those who do not believe Jesus Christ has come in the flesh, These have gone out to deceive.
1:8	That's the deceiver, antichrist. So "Watch out!" *I've underscored. Don't lose what we have accomplished, But receive your full reward.
1:9	Any person who runs ahead But no longer does abide In the teaching that Christ has taught Does not have God inside.
	If one continues abiding In what the Christ has taught, Then both the Father and the Son This one has truly got.
1:10	If one does not bring this teaching Who comes to your church meeting,* Do not welcome him in your house. Do not give him a greeting.
1:11	He who gives him a greeting Is a participant With him in his evil teachings, Regardless of the intent.*

1:12   I've many things I'd like to say,
Yet not by letters or scripts.[84]
I wish to come to you and speak
With words from my own lips.

I hope to speak to you face to face
That your joy may be complete.
1:13   The children of your chosen sister,
You they all do greet.

THIRD JOHN

1:1   This is written by the elder
      To my beloved friend,
      To Gaius whom I truly love.
      This letter to you I send.*

1:2   I pray, beloved, that in all ways
      Your health is sound and whole,
      That you succeed in every way
      In the same way as your soul.

1:3   For I was very glad to hear
      How in the truth you live
      When brothers came and testified
      To the living truth you give.

1:4   I have no greater joy than this:
      When of my children I hear
      That they are living in the truth,
      To the truth they do adhere.*

1:5   You act faithfully, my dear friend,
      In whatever work you do
      On behalf of fellow brothers,
      Even if strangers to you.

1:6   Before the church they've testified
Of the love you display.
So, in a manner pleasing God,
Send them on their way.

1:7   For they travel for a reason,
For the sake of the Name,
Accepting nothing from Gentiles,
Not looking for any gain.*

1:8   Therefore, we must support such men,
For when we pay this price,*
We become coworkers in truth
With these who sacrifice.*

1:9   I've written something to the church,
But one hates what we proclaim,
Who lusts for headship of the church.
Diotrephes is his name.

1:10   Because of this, if I should come,
His works I will point out,
Like slandering us with evil words,
Spreading his lies about.*

And not content with just these things,
The brethren he won't receive,
And those who wish to welcome them,
From the church he makes them leave.

1:11   Do not mimic what is evil,
Gaius, my dear friend,
But only mimic what is good.
For good always contend.*

>   He who has the lifestyle of good,
>   To God he does belong.
>   Nobody has ever seen God
>   That has a lifestyle of wrong.
>
> **1:12**   Demetrius is approved by all
>   And by the truth as well.
>   We approve of Demetrius,
>   And you know the truth we tell.
>
> **1:13**   I've many things I'd like to say,
>   Yet not by letters or scripts;[85]
> **1:14**   I will see you shortly and speak
>   With words from my own lips.
>
>   "Peace to you!" *is now what I write.
>   The friends here send a greeting.
>   Greet by name the friends you have there.
>   Soon we will be meeting.*

THE POETIC REVELATION TO JOHN

1:1 The Revelation from Jesus Christ,
Which to Him God did entrust
To show His servants sudden events,
And come suddenly[86] they must.

Jesus sent and communicated,
This revelation God gave,
Through His angelic messenger
To John, His chosen bond slave.

1:2 His bond slave, John, has testified
Of God's word that he was told
And of Jesus Christ's testimony,
Of all that he did behold.

1:3 Blessed is the one who keeps on reading
The prophetic words they see,
And blessed are those who keep on hearing
This written prophecy.

Blessed are those who keep on obeying
All that's been written here
In this record of Revelation,
For the time[87] is very near.

1:4   This record has been written by John,
And to these it has been sent:
To the churches which are in Asia.
To seven of them it went.

Grace and peace has been given to you!
A divine source this is from,
From Him who is and who's always been
And who's also yet to come.

And it is from the seven Spirits
Who exist before His throne,
1:5   And also it is from Jesus Christ
Whose character has been shown.*

Jesus Christ is the faithful witness,
The firstborn over the dead,
Ruler over the kings of the earth,
And for us His blood He shed.

To Him who loves[88] us unselfishly
And released us from our sins
By means of His blood He shed for us.
All our wrongs He did cleanse.

1:6   He has made us to be a kingdom,
To His God and Father, priests.
To Him is the glory and the power,
Amen, it will never cease.

1:7	Behold! He is coming with the clouds
And Him every eye will see,
Even unbelievers who pierced Him,
For He will return visibly.

Over Him all earthly tribes will mourn
When they see Him come again.
They will lament over His return,
And so it will be, amen. |
| 1:8 | "I'm the Alpha and the Omega,
The Lord God, the Almighty One,
Him who is and who has always been
And who's also yet to come." |
| 1:9 | I, John, your brother and companion,
In Jesus I share with you
The tribulation and the kingdom
And patient endurance too.

Because I preached the word of God
And testified of Jesus,
I was put on the island, Patmos,
Which is south of Miletus.* |
| 1:10 | By the Spirit I was inspired
On a certain Lord's day,
When behind me I heard a loud voice,
A voice like a trumpet say: |
| 1:11 | "Write down all that you see in a scroll,
And to these churches send
The Revelation you recorded
That they may comprehend. |

"Send it to Ephesus and to Smyrna.
Send it to Pergamum too,
To Thyatira and to Sardis.
Send it you must do.*

"Send this book to Philadelphia,
And send it to one more.*
Send this book to Laodicea.
Seven churches it is for."

1:12   I turned to see who was the speaker.
This is what caught my eye:
There were these seven golden lampstands
And someone standing by.

1:13   He stood in the midst of the lampstands.
He was like a son of man,
Clothed with a robe reaching to His feet,
And across His chest, a gold band.

1:14   His head and hair were extremely white,
As white as white wool and snow.
His eyes were like a flame of fire,
1:15   And His feet, how they did glow!

They looked as if they were burnished bronze
Heated in a refinery.
Like rushing waters His voice sounded,
1:16   And seven stars I could see.

In His right hand He held seven stars,
And jutting out of His mouth
Was a long, sharp, double-edged sword.
His face, like the sun, shined out.

The Poetic Revelation to John

1:17 I fell at His feet when I saw Him.
I fell as if I were dead,
But He laid His right hand upon me,
And this is what He said:

"Do not fear. I'm the First and the Last.
1:18 I am the Living One.
I was dead, but behold I'm alive,
And I will live on and on.

"I have the keys of death and Hades.
1:19 So write down all that you see;
Record the things which were and which are
and all the things that will be.

1:20 "As for the mystery of the stars
Which you saw in My right hand
And the seven lampstands of gold,
Listen and understand.

"The seven stars are the messengers[89]
Of the seven churches, indeed.
The seven lampstands made of gold
Are the seven churches *they lead.

2:1 "Write to the Ephesus messenger[90]
Who leads the church that is there;
Write down all the words that I dictate;
Write all the words I declare.

"The One who clenches the seven stars
Firmly within His right hand,
Who walks among the seven lampstands,
Says this to understand:

2:2 "I commend you for the deeds you do.
You toil and persevere.
You cannot put up with evil men;
Them you do not revere.

"I commend you for applying tests
To those who have proclaimed
That they themselves are apostles,
But *false* by you they're named.

2:3 "I commend you for persevering,
For enduring for My name.
You've not grown weary in your deeds.
In these things you have no blame.

2:4 "But this is what I have against you:
Your first love you've forsaken.
2:5 So remember where you've fallen from.
Your first deeds now awaken.

"Repent and do the first deeds you did,
Or else to you I will come
And remove your lampstand from its place,
Unless repentance is done.

2:6 "I do commend you for one more deed:
These works you don't tolerate,
The deeds of the Nicolaitans
Whose actions I also hate.

2:7 "The one who has an ear to listen,
Hear what the Spirit does say,
For He is speaking to the churches.
Listen, apply, and obey.[91]

"To the one who overcomes with faith,
I'll give to him without price
To eat the fruit of the tree of life
That's in God's paradise.

2:8 "Write to the messenger in Smyrna
Who leads the church that is there;
Write down all the words that I dictate;
Write all the words I declare.

"The One who is the First and the Last,
Who was dead some time ago,
But now is resurrected to life,
Says this for you to know:

2:9 "I know the tribulation you have.
In poverty you've been pitched,
But although you are so very poor,
You're spiritually enriched.

"I know that you are being blasphemed
By those who say they are Jews,
But they're a synagogue of Satan.
Of themselves they have false views.*

2:10   "Do not fear what you soon will suffer.
　　　　　The Devil will soon assail.
　　　　　He will cast some of you in prison
　　　　　To tempt you so you might fail.

　　　　　"Ten days you will have tribulation.
　　　　　You must endure this strife.*
　　　　　Be faithful until the time you die,
　　　　　And I'll give you the crown[92] of life.

2:11   "The one who has an ear to listen,
　　　　　Hear what the Spirit does say,
　　　　　For He is speaking to the churches.
　　　　　Listen, apply, and obey.

　　　　　"To the one who overcomes with faith,
　　　　　Though he may draw his last breath,*
　　　　　This one will never ever be hurt
　　　　　By the second death.

2:12   "Write to the Pergamum messenger
　　　　　Who leads the church that is there;
　　　　　Write down all the words that I dictate;
　　　　　Write all the words I declare.

　　　　　"The One who has coming from His mouth
　　　　　A long, sharp, double-edged sword,
　　　　　Says this so that your activity
　　　　　Would with Me be in accord:*

2:13   "I am well aware of where you live,
        Where Satan has his throne.
        I praise you for holding fast My name.
        My faith you did not disown.

        "Even in the days of Antipas,
        My witness, My faithful one,
        When he was killed where Satan dwells,
        Your faith could not be undone.

2:14   "But a few things I have against you.
        There are those you tolerate
        Who hold to the teaching of Balaam,
        Whose teaching I deeply hate.

        "He kept teaching Balak to entice
        The sons of Israel, who fell,
        To eat things sacrificed to idols,
        To fornicate as well.

2:15   "The other thing I have against you,
        You have some there who follow
        What the Nicolaitans teach,
        Which teaching none should swallow.*

2:16   "I will come to you in suddenness.[93]
        Repent I say, therefore,
        Or else with the sword from My mouth
        I will with them make war.

2:17   "The one who has an ear to listen,
        Hear what the Spirit does say,
        For He is speaking to the churches.
        Listen, apply, and obey.

"To the one who overcomes with faith
I'll give two things that are white,[94]
Of the hidden manna and a stone,
And on this stone I will write.

"There he will have a new name inscribed
That by others won't be known.
The only one who will know this name
Is the one who gets that stone.

2:18   "Write to Thyatira's messenger
Who leads the church that is there.
Write down all the words that I dictate;
Write all the words I declare.

"The Son of God, whose eyes are like fire,
Whose feet are all aglow
Which look as if they are burnished bronze,
Says this for you to know:

2:19   "I commend you for the deeds you do.
They have these qualities:
Unselfish love[95] and faith and service
And patience of high degrees.

"I commend you for the deeds you do
Which are greater than at first,
2:20   But this is what I have against you,
Which deed must be reversed:*

"You tolerate an evil woman.
Jezebel is her name.
She calls herself a prophetess,
Which is a lying claim.*

"She teaches and leads My bond slaves astray
So that they fornicate
And eat foods sacrificed to idols.
These I can't tolerate.*

2:21 "I gave her enough time to repent
Of her fornication.
Since she is unwilling to repent,
2:22 I'll give her tribulation.

"Behold, I will throw her on a bed,
A bed of fornication.
Those who join her in adultery
I'll give great tribulation.

"If they do not repent of her deeds,
This I will surely do,
2:23 And I will strike her children with death
Since her deeds they pursue.*

"All the churches will know I'm the One
Who searches each heart and mind,
And I will give to each one of you
According to your deeds I find.

2:24 "The rest of you in Thyatira,
This doctrine you refuse.
You've not known the 'deep things' of Satan,
Which is the term they use.

	"To you I say, no other burden
	On your shoulders I will lay,
2:25	But keep a firm hold on what you have
	Until I come on that day.

2:26 "To the one who overcomes with faith,
Who keeps My deeds 'til the end,
To him I will give authority
Over nations which will bend.

2:27 "And that one will rule all the nations
With a strong iron rod,
Like the potter's broken clay vessels,
With pieces scattered abroad.

"This was given Me by My Father:
To rule with an iron bar.
To those who overcome I'll give that
2:28 And also the morning star.

2:29 "The one who has an ear to listen,
Hear what the Spirit does say,
For He is speaking to the churches.
Listen, apply, and obey.

3:1 "Write to the messenger in Sardis
Who leads the church that is there;
Write down all the words that I dictate;
Write all the words I declare.

"The One who has the seven Spirits
Who exist before God's throne,[96]
The One who has the seven stars,
Has these words to make known:

"I'm well aware of all your deeds.
For yourselves you've made a name.
To others you look very alive,
But you're dead, I proclaim.

3:2   "Wake up and strengthen that which remains,
For they are about to die.
I have not found your deeds completed
In My God's very eye.

3:3   "Therefore, remember what you've received.
Remember all that you've heard.
Repent from the deadness of your deeds,
And hold firmly to My word.

"Now if you don't wake up from your deeds,
I will arrive like a thief.
You'll have no sign when I come to you,
Not even a warning that's brief.*

3:4   "You have a few people in Sardis
Who have not soiled their clothes.
They will walk with Me dressed in white
Because of great worth are those.

3:5   "The one who overcomes with faith
Will wear clothes in this way:
Having garments unsoiled and white.
That will be the array.

"That one's name is in the book of life,
Whose name I'll never erase.
I'll confess it before God's angels,
And before My Father's face.

3:6 "The one who has an ear to listen,
Hear what the Spirit does say.
For He is speaking to the churches.
Listen, apply, and obey.

3:7 "For the Philadelphia messenger
Who leads the church that is there,
Write down all the words that I dictate;
Write all the words I declare.

"The holy, true One has David's key.
What He opens none will close,
And what He shuts no one can open.
These words He does propose:

3:8 "I'm well aware of all your deeds.
Look at the door before you.
I've opened that door which none can close,
I who am holy and true.

"For these reasons this door is for you:
A little strength you have gained,
Faithful you are in keeping My word,
And My name you've not disclaimed.

3:9

"Look! From the synagogue of Satan,
I'll give these ones to you.
These are the ones who say they are Jews,
But they lie! It's not true!

"I will cause them to come before you,
And to worship at your feet.
They will realize that I have loved you.
I'll save them from their deceit.*

3:10

"Because you've faithfully kept My word,
To endure and persevere,
I'll also keep you from what's to come,
An hour that is severe.

"This time will impact the entire world.
This time is about to birth.
It will be an hour of trials and tests
For those who live on the earth.

3:11

"Behold, I am coming suddenly.[97]
Hold fast to what you own
So that no one will receive[98] the crown[99]
That was meant for you alone.

3:12

"The one who overcomes with faith,
A pillar I'll make him to be.
He'll be in the temple of My God,
Staying there permanently.

"I'll write on him the name of My God,
The name of His city too
(The new Jerusalem from heaven),
Also My name that is new.

3:13 "The one who has an ear to listen,
Hear what the Spirit does say.
For He is speaking to the churches.
Listen, apply, and obey.

3:14 "The Laodicea messenger
Who leads the church that is there,
Write him all the words that I dictate.
Write him all that I declare.

"The One who is the Amen, the truth,[100]
The witness who's faithful and true,
The ruler[101] over God's creation,
That One says this to you:

3:15 "I know your deeds, every one of them,
That you're neither cold nor hot.
I wish you were one or the other,
But either one you're not.

3:16 "So since you are neither hot nor cold
But are only just lukewarm,
I will vomit you out of My mouth
So that your lives will transform.*

3:17 "You say, 'I am rich and wealthy.'
'I have no needs,' you've stressed.
You don't know that you're wretched, and poor,
Miserable, blind, and undressed.

The Poetic Revelation to John

3:18
"Since you have boasted of the wrong things,
I urge you from Me to buy
Gold that has been refined by fire.
Be rich in what I supply.

"I urge you to buy from Me white clothes
That you may put them on
So that the shame of your nakedness
Will not be exposed, but gone.

"I urge you to buy from Me ointment
For you to anoint your eyes
So that you may be able to see.
That is what I advise.

3:19
"Those whom I love with deep affection[102]
I reprove and discipline.
Eagerly turn from being lukewarm.
Let your repentance begin.

3:20
"Behold, I stand knocking at the door.
If anyone hears My voice
And opens the door, I will come in,
And we will dine and rejoice.

3:21
"I'll grant the one who overcomes
To sit with Me on My throne
Just as I conquered and was seated
With My Father alone.

3:22
"The one who has an ear to listen,
Hear what the Spirit does say.
For He is speaking to the churches.
Listen, apply, and obey."

4:1 After this revelation Christ gave,
I looked and this caught my eye:
A door that was standing wide open
Which was in heaven on high.

The same voice who had spoken to me
Like that of a trumpeter
Said, "Come up here and I will show you
After this what must occur."

4:2 Suddenly, in the Spirit I was,
And there in heaven on high,
Behold there was this heavenly throne.
He who sat on it caught my eye.

4:3 The One who sat had this appearance:
A jasper and sardius stone,
And a rainbow, like an emerald,
Was wrapped around the throne.

4:4 Around this throne were twenty-four thrones.
Twenty-four elders sat there.
On their heads they had crowns[103] of gold,
And white clothes they did wear.

4:5 From the throne came thunder and lightning
And sounds *that were bizarre.
Before the throne seven fire lamps burned.
God's seven Spirits these are.

4:6	In front of the throne was a sea of glass
	That had crystal-like features.
	In the center and around the throne
	There were four living creatures.
	These living creatures were filled with eyes
	In front and also behind.
	Each had distinct appearances
	Like creatures of these kind:
4:7	The first creature looked like a lion,
	The second like a calf, all right.
	The third had a face like a human,
	The fourth like an eagle in flight.
4:8	Now each one of them possessed six wings,
	Covered completely with eyes.
	Day and night they continually said
	These praises, repeating their cries:
	"Holy, holy, holy is the Lord.
	He's God, the Almighty One.
	He's Him who is, who has always been,
	And who's also yet to come."
4:9	This honor and thanks they give to Him
	Who's sitting upon the throne,
	The One who lives on forevermore.
	They give praise to Him alone.*
	And when they give Him honor and thanks,
4:10	The twenty-four elders respond
	To the One who sits upon the throne
	And lives forever beyond.

They respond, falling down before Him,
And before the throne they lay
Their crowns of gold that were on their heads,
And to Him they all do say:

4:11   "You are worthy, our Lord and our God,
To receive from Your creation
Glory, honor, and all the power,
And praise without cessation.*

"For You have created everything.
All things exist by Your will.
And by it all things were created
For Your purpose to fulfill."

5:1   I saw a scroll in that One's right hand
Who on the throne did sit.
Writing was on both sides of the scroll
With seven seals around it.

5:2   A mighty angel with a loud voice,
This decree I watched him make:
"Who is worthy to open the scroll,
And the seals of it to break?"

5:3   Not one could even open the scroll.
Not one could look inside,
Not one in heaven or on the earth,
Or anyone who had died.

5:4	I deeply wept in response to this.
	Worthiness could not be found
	To open the scroll or look inside.
	The scroll was forever bound.*
5:5	Then one of the elders said to me,
	"Stop weeping, but look and see!
	The Lion from the tribe of Judah,
	David's Root, won victory.
	"This One has finally overcome
	So as to open the scroll.
	Its seven seals He can release.
	Yes, it He can unroll."
5:6	I saw standing in between the throne
	(With the four living creatures),
	Between the throne and the elders,
	A Lamb who had these features:
	The Lamb was standing as if slaughtered.
	This One had won the prize.*
	Upon His head there were seven horns,
	And on His face, seven eyes.
	The seven eyes that were on His face
	Denote, on this One of worth,[104]
	The seven Spirits of the one God
	Sent out into all the earth.
5:7	He approached Him who sat on the throne.
	The worthy One took the scroll.
	He took it out of His right hand,
	Causing heaven to extol.

| 5:8 | For when the Lamb had taken the scroll,
A response it did impel:
Four living creatures, twenty-four elders,
Before the Lamb just fell.

The living creatures and the elders,
Each had a harp in their hand.
They had golden bowls full of incense
(For the saints' prayers these stand). |
|---|---|
| 5:9 | They sang a new song that went like this:
"You are truly of great worth
To take the scroll and release its seals
Because of Your work on earth.*

"You were slain, and You purchased for God,
With Your own blood that was spilled,
From every tribe, tongue, clan, and nation.
For those people You were killed. |
| 5:10 | "Those You purchased You have made,
You who as a lamb was slain,
To be both kings and priests to our God,
And on the earth they will reign." |
| 5:11 | I looked and heard many angels sing.
They were all around the throne.
They sang with the creatures and elders
In a sweet, melodic tone.*

There were ten thousand times ten thousand,
And thousands of thousands more,
Countless angels sang with the others.
To the Lamb this song was for: |

5:12	"Worthy is the Lamb who was slain To receive now and always Power and wealth and wisdom and might, Honor and glory and praise."
5:13	And every created thing joined in Who on earth or in heaven abide, All those on the sea and those within, Even all those who had died. They sang, "To Him who sits on the throne And to the Lamb we adore, Be blessing and honor and glory, And power forevermore."
5:14	The living creatures kept repeating. "Amen, amen," was their word, And the elders fell down and worshipped. All this I saw and heard.*

6:1	I watched as the Lamb released one seal. Then a thunderous voice I heard From one of the four living creatures. "Go!"[105] was the creature's word.
6:2	And then I saw a white horse go out. Its rider had a great bow. A victory wreath[106] was given him. On a conquest he did go.

6:3 When a second seal the Lamb released,
Another voice I heard.
A second living creature spoke.
"Go!" was that creature's word.

6:4 Another horse, a red one, went out,
Its rider given a great sword,
Granted power to take peace from earth
So that men just killed and warred.

6:5 Now when a third seal the Lamb released,
A different voice I heard.
A third living creature had spoken.
"Go!" was this creature's word.

And I looked and there was a black horse.
Its rider held scales in his hand,
6:6 And among the four living creatures
A voice issued this command:

"You're not to harm the oil nor the wine.
The price of this will be due:
One day's wages for a quart of wheat,
For three quarts of barley too."

6:7 And when a fourth seal the Lamb released,
Another voice I heard.
The fourth living creature had spoken.
"Go!" was that creature's word.

6:8 I looked and there was a pale green horse.
Death was its rider's name.
Hades followed him as he went out.
This power they could claim:

	Power over one-fourth of the world
	To kill with sword and dearth,[107]
	And to kill with plagues that are carried[108]
	By the wild beasts of the earth.

6:9   And when a fifth seal the Lamb released,
Under the altar I viewed
The lives of those who had been martyred
Due to the life they pursued.

They kept obeying the word of God.
Their testimony was pure,
But they were killed for their faithfulness.
Until death they did endure.*

6:10   The martyrs cried out with a loud voice,
"O Lord, You're holy and true!
How long will You not judge or avenge
Our blood we spilled for You?"

6:11   Each one of them was given a robe.
A white robe they were to wear.
They were told to continue to rest
For a little longer there.

For they had to wait 'til others died,
Their fellow servants and brothers.
More were to be martyred as they were.
They were to wait for these others.

6:12   And when a sixth seal the Lamb released,
A great shaking then took place.
The sun turned black as sackcloth of hair.
Like blood was the moon's face.

6:13	The stars of the sky fell to the earth,
	And, oh, how they did descend,
	Like a fig tree casting unripe figs
	When shaken by a great wind.
6:14	Like a scroll when it is all rolled up,
	The sky then did divide.
	Every mountain and island were moved
	From the place they occupied.
6:15	The kings of the earth and the rulers,
	The generals, the rich, and strong,
	Every slave and every free person,
	All knew they had done wrong.*
	They hid themselves in the caves they found
	And by the mountains' boulders.
6:16	They cried to the mountains and the rocks
	To hide *their head and shoulders.
	They cried out, "Fall on us and hide us
	From Him who sits on the throne;
	Hide us from His terrible presence.
	We do not wish to be shown."
	They cried out, "Fall on us and hide us
	From the Lamb's wrath we demand,
6:17	For the great day of their wrath has come,
	And who is able to stand?"

The Poetic Revelation to John

7:1   After all this I saw four angels
At the earth's four corners stand,
Holding back the four winds of the earth
So no wind blew on the land.

No wind blew on the land or the sea
Or any tree; it had ceased.
7:2   Then I saw another angel
Coming up from the east.

This angel held the living God's seal,
And ordered the other four
Who were given the power to harm
The earth and the sea and more.

7:3   "Do not harm neither the sea nor trees.
Upon earth bring no ordeal
'Til on the foreheads of God's bond slaves
We've finished placing God's seal."

7:4   Now one hundred forty-four thousand
With the seal of God were sealed,
From every tribe of Israel's sons.
I heard this number revealed.

7:5   Twelve thousand from each of the twelve tribes
Were sealed after this decree,
The tribes of Judah, Reuben, and Gad,
7:6   Asher and Naphtali.

7:7	Those of Manasseh and Simeon,
	Levi and Issachar,
7:8	Joseph, Zebulin, and Benjamin,
	All sealed these tribes now are.*
7:9	After these things I looked and beheld
	A great crowd which none could count
	From every nation, tribe, clan, and tongue,
	An innumerable amount.
	Before the throne and before the Lamb
	Was standing this great crowd.
	They all had palm branches in their hands.
	With white robes they were endowed.
7:10	I heard them cry out with a loud voice.
	In unison they began,
	"Salvation to our God on the throne,
	And salvation to the Lamb."
7:11	All the angels stood around the throne,
	The four living creatures too,
	And the elders stood around the throne
	As this they began to do:
	They all fell down upon their faces,
	And worshipped God on the throne,
7:12	"Truly all these things belong to You,
	And belong to You alone:*
	"Blessing and glory, wisdom and thanks,
	Honor and power and might,
	To our God forever and ever,
	Amen," they did recite.

7:13   And one of the elders questioned me,
        "Those in white robes over there,
        Just who are they and whence have they come?
        Tell me the who and the where."

7:14   I said, "My dear sir, you know; tell me."
        Their origin he went on to state,
        "These are the ones who come out of this:
        The tribulation that's great."

        Then he told me their identity,
        And this is what he said:
        "These are they who have made their robes white
        In the Lamb's blood that was shed.

7:15   "Because of this they're before God's throne,
        And they serve God day and night.
        They keep serving Him in His temple,
        And they never leave His sight.*

        "And He who is seated on the throne,
        His tent over them He'll place.
7:16   They will never hunger anymore,
        Or thirst in any case.

        "The sun will never beat down on them,
        Or any scorching heat
7:17   Because in the center of the throne
        Is the Lamb who did defeat.[109]

        "The Lamb will always be their shepherd.
        To living spring waters He'll guide.
        From their eyes God will wipe away tears;
        Sorrow from them He will hide."*

8:1   And when the last seal the Lamb released,
Silence there was in heaven.
It lasted about one-half an hour.
It was seal number seven.

8:2   And I could see the seven angels
Who before God always stand,
And they were given seven trumpets
To sound at God's command.*

8:3   Then another angel came and stood
At the altar seen before,
Holding a golden incense burner,
And given incense galore.

It was given so that he could add
To what all the saints have prayed.
On the gold altar before the throne,
The incense and prayers were laid.

8:4   The smoke of the incense rose up high.
With the saints' prayers it went
Before God out of the angel's hand.
From the altar these were sent.

8:5   The angel took the incense burner.
With the altar's fire he filled,
And then threw it down onto the earth.
The half hour was fulfilled.*

	Peals of thunder and sounds then followed,

           Peals of thunder and sounds then followed,
           Lightning strikes and a quake.
8:6   The seven angels with the trumpets
           Prepared their sounds to make.

8:7   The first angel sounded his trumpet—
           Hail and fire were produced.
           Mixed with blood these were thrown to the earth.
           To ashes things were reduced.

           One-third of the earth was burned right up.
           One-third of the trees were too,
           And all of the green grass was consumed.
           No green grass was in view.*

8:8   The second one sounded his trumpet—
           Then there appeared to be
           Something like a great mountain on fire
           That was thrown into the sea.

           Then one-third of the sea became blood.
8:9   One-third of all sea life died,
           And one-third of the ships were destroyed
           That on the sea did ride.

8:10   The third angel sounded his trumpet—
           A great star fell from the sky.
           Like a burning torch it came down,
           Hitting the water supply.[110]

           It fell on one-third of the rivers,
           One-third of the well springs too.
8:11   The name of the star is called Wormwood,
           And wormwood became the brew.

One-third of the waters turned bitter
So that many people died
By drinking from rivers and well springs
Where Wormwood did collide.

8:12 The fourth angel sounded his trumpet—
Sun, moon, and stars were lit.
One-third of the sun, one-third of the moon,
And one-third of the stars were hit.

One-third of the day would become dark,
The sun unseen at that time.
One-third of the night there'd be no light
Since no moon nor stars would shine.

8:13 I looked and in the midst of the sky
An eagle came into sight.
He was announcing in a loud voice
This warning while in flight:

"Three woes to those who live on the earth
Since these three are the last.
Three more angels will announce these woes.
Their trumpets are soon to blast."

9:1 The fifth angel sounded his trumpet—
And I was able to see
A star fallen from heaven to earth,
And the angel given a key.

	The key was to the bottomless pit.
9:2	The angel opened the pit,
	And like the smoke of a great furnace
	Smoke came up out of it.

	The smoke darkened the sun and the sky
	As it rose from the deep hole.
9:3	Out of the smoke locusts swarmed the earth,
	Given a certain control.

	Their power was like earthly scorpions.
9:4	They were told not to harm these:
	The earth's grass or any greenery
	Or any of earth's trees.

They only had the power to hurt
Those who did not possess
The seal of God on their foreheads.
Only those they could distress.

9:5 They weren't allowed to kill anyone.
For five months their harm would span.
Their hurt would be like a scorpion
When a scorpion stings a man.

9:6 Now in those days people will seek death,
Yet death on them won't fall.
They will desire to die and not live,
But death will flee from them all.

9:7 The locusts had a strange appearance,
Like horses prepared for war.
There was something they had on their heads.
It was gold wreath-like décor.[111]

	Their faces were like human faces.
9:8	They had hair like women's hair.
	Their teeth were like the teeth of lions,
9:9	And breastplates they did wear.

        They had breastplates like that of iron.
        The sound of their wings were loud,
        Like rushing horses and chariots
        Producing a battle cloud.

9:10   They had tails like that of scorpions,
        And stings without relief.
        For five months their tails had the power
        To hurt those in unbelief.

9:11   They have a king that rules over them,
        The angel of the abyss.
        His name is Abaddon in Hebrew.
        Apollyon is Greek for this.

9:12   This is the first woe that now is past,
        But there is more yet to come.
        Still on the way there are two more woes
        After the first woe is done.

9:13   The sixth angel sounded his trumpet—
        Then I heard a voice command
        From the four horns of the gold altar
        Which before God does stand.

9:14   The voice commanded the sixth angel
        That had made his trumpet sound,
        "Release from the great river Euphrates
        The four angels that are bound."

9:15 These four had been prepared for this time,
    This hour, day, month, and year,
    Released to kill one-third of mankind.
    Death they would engineer.*

9:16 The number of the horsemen's armies—
    Two hundred million, I heard.
9:17 The vision of these horses and riders
    I saw and describe by this word:

    The riders had breastplates of fire,
    Of hyacinth and brimstone.
    The horses' heads were like lion heads,
    And plagues from their mouths were thrown.

    Out of their mouths three plagues proceeded,
    Fire and smoke and brimstone.
9:18 One-third of man was killed by these plagues
    That from their mouths were thrown.

9:19 For in their mouths, also in their tails,
    Were the power of the horses.
    Their tails were like serpents having heads,
    Inflicting painful forces.

9:20 The rest of mankind who were not killed
    By the three plagues that fell
    Did not repent from their handiworks,
    But continued to rebel.

    They did not stop worshipping demons,
    Or idols of silver or gold,
    Or idols of brass or stone or wood,
    Which have no power to hold.

| | They continued to worship idols
Which can't walk or hear or see, |
| 9:21 | Not turning from murders, witchcraft, thefts,
Or sexual immorality. |

| 10:1 | Another strong angel I then saw
From heaven coming down.
The clothing he wore was just a cloud,
And a rainbow was his crown. |

| | His face was like the sun when it shines,
Like pillars of fire, his feet. |
| 10:2 | He had in his hand a little scroll
Unrolled as a single sheet. |

| | He placed his right foot on the sea.
His left on the land he set. |
| 10:3 | Then he cried out in a mighty voice
Like a lion roaring a threat. |

| | Then the seven peals of thunder spoke,
In their sounds speaking a word. |
| 10:4 | While listening to what they were saying,
I began to write what I heard. |

| | But then a voice from heaven I heard,
"Keep these things secret," it said.
"What the seven peals of thunder spoke,
Don't write; they must not be read."* |

10:5	And the angel whom I saw standing (Standing on the sea and land) Swore by the One who lives forever By lifting up his right hand.
10:6	To heaven he raised his hand and swore By Him from whom all things stem, Who made the heavens, earth, and sea, And all that is within them.
10:7	He swore there would be no more delay, For the day is about to come When the seventh angel starts to sound. Then it will all be done.
	The mystery of God will be fulfilled. This day will not be denied* As He preached to His servants, the prophets, Who in turn then prophesied.
10:8	Then the voice which I heard from heaven Issued me this command: "Obtain the scroll in the angel's hand Who stands on the sea and land."
10:9	I went to the angel, telling him To give me the little scroll, But he told me, "Take it and eat it, Not in part, but the whole.
	"In your stomach the scroll will become Bitter to a great degree, But in your mouth the scroll will taste sweet Like honey from a bee."

10:10	The little scroll in the angel's hand,
	I took it, and then I ate.
	In my mouth it was sweet as honey.
	In my stomach, a sour state.
10:11	They said to me, "You must prophesy
	Again of many things
	Concerning many nations and clans
	And many tongues and kings."

11:1	I was given a measuring reed
	That looked something like a rod,
	And then someone told me to measure
	The sanctuary[112] of God.
	"Rise and measure God's sanctuary.
	Measure the altar too,
	And measure those who worship in it,
11:2	But this you must not do:
	"You must not measure the outer court.
	In the Gentiles'[113] hands it's been put.
	They will trample for forty-two months
	The holy city underfoot.
11:3	"To my two witnesses I will grant
	The power to prophesy.
	They'll do this twelve hundred sixty days.
	In sackcloth they'll testify."

11:4   These prophets are the two olive trees
And the two lampstands that stand
In the presence of the Lord of the earth.
They'll travel throughout the land.*

11:5   Fire can proceed out of their mouth.
So if any who has willed
To inflict harm upon these prophets,
By fire they will be killed.

11:6   The prophets have the authority
To shut up the whole sky,
To keep the rain from falling on earth
In the days they prophesy.

These prophets have the authority
With all plagues the earth to strike
And to turn the waters into blood
As often as they might like.

11:7   When they have finished testifying,
From the pit[114] will come the beast
To attack and overpower them
Until life in them has ceased.

11:8   There will lie in the great city's street
The bodies of these who died,
Mystically called Sodom and Egypt,
Where their Lord was crucified.

11:9   Their dead bodies will be viewed by those
From clans, tribes, tongues, and nations.
For three and one-half days they will view
With many celebrations.

| | They won't permit their lifeless bodies
| | To be laid in any grave,
| **11:10** | And these ones that live upon the earth
| | Will joy over them and rave.

| | They will engage in celebrations.
| | Gifts they'll receive and give
| | Because these two prophets tormented
| | Those on the earth who live.

11:11 But after those three and one-half days,
God gave them life-giving breath.
Great fear struck those who saw them standing
Triumphant over death.

11:12 Then they heard a loud voice from heaven.
"Come up here," was its call.
They went up to heaven in a cloud,
Their enemies seeing it all.

11:13 A great earthquake occurred at that time.
One-tenth of the city did fall.
Many people were killed in the quake,
Seven thousand people in all.

And the rest of those who were not killed,
They became terrified.
So they turned to the God of heaven,
And Him they glorified.

11:14 This is the second woe that is past,
But there's one more yet to come.
The third woe is coming suddenly[115]
When the second is all done.

11:15 The seventh angel blew his trumpet—
Loud voices from heaven did ring,
"This world's kingdom has become our Lord's
And His Christ's, *who is the King.

"Christ is the King, the Anointed One,[116]
Who will now begin to reign.
He will rule forever and ever!"
These voices did proclaim.

11:16 The twenty-four elders, who do sit
Before God upon their thrones,
Fell on their faces in His presence,
Saying in worshipful tones:

11:17 "Thank You, O Lord, God the Almighty,
Who is and who's always been,
For You have taken Your great power
So Your reign can now begin.

11:18 "Then the nations became furious,
And Your wrath came about.
It was time for the dead to be judged
And rewards to be given out.

"The time came to reward Your bond slaves,
The prophets and the saints,
The small and the great who fear Your name.
And there were no complaints.*

"But to those who are not Your bond slaves,
Time came to judge their worth.
Time came to destroy all those who were
The corrupters of the earth."

11:19 God's sanctuary[117] was opened up
       (The one in heaven, I mean).
       The ark of His covenant was there
       So as to be easily seen.

       There were flashes of lightning and sounds.
       Peals of thunder did form.
       There was also a great big shaking,
       And a tremendous hailstorm.

12:1   Now a great sign appeared in heaven,
       Someone clothed with the sun,
       And right under the feet was the moon.
       A woman was this one.

       On her head was a wreath[118] of twelve stars,
12:2   And she was no doubt with child.
       Then being in labor, she cried out.
       The labor pains were not mild.

12:3   Another sign appeared in heaven,
       A dragon, enormous and red.
       It possessed seven heads and ten horns
       With a royal crown[119] on each head.

12:4   His powerful tail then swept away
       One-third of the stars in the sky,
       Which he threw down to the earth below.
       Then before her he stood by.

As the woman began to give birth,
Over her he did tower
So that when she delivered her child,
The child he could devour.

12:5 She finally gave birth to a son,
A male with a plan from God.
He was to rule over all nations
With an iron rod.

Her child was snatched up to God's presence
And brought before His throne.
12:6 The woman ran into the desert
To a place that was her own.

For God had prepared a special place
So that there she could be fed
One thousand two hundred sixty days.
She was nourished where she fled.

12:7 Now a battle occurred in heaven.
Michael and his angels fought
Against the dragon and his angels.
But win the demons could not.

12:8 For the great dragon and his angels
Lacked enough strength on their side,
And there was no longer in heaven
A place for them to abide.

12:9 The enormous dragon was thrown down,
Who is the Serpent of old,
Also known as the Devil and Satan.
His place he could not hold.

Now he does hold this kind of power:*
To deceive the entire world,
For he has been thrown down to the earth.
With his angels he's been hurled.

12:10 Then in heaven I heard a loud voice,
"Salvation has finally come.
The power and kingdom of our God
Has arrived *because of His Son.

"His Christ now has His authority.
The accuser has been hurled,
Who night and day accused before God
Our brothers in the world.

12:11 "The accuser they have overcome
Due to the Lamb's blood that was shed
And due to the word of their witness
They kept until they were dead.

"For they did not cherish their own lives
Even in the face of death.
The word of their witness they preserved*
Until they drew their last breath.*

12:12 "For this reason rejoice, O heavens
And all you who in them dwell,
But woe to the earth and to the sea,
For to earth the Devil fell.

"Since he has been cast out of heaven,
He has come down to you all.
He is possessing tremendous wrath,
Knowing his season is small."

12:13	When the dragon realized where he was,
	Being thrown down to the earth,
	He pursued the woman of the male
	To whom she had given birth.
12:14	But the two wings of the great eagle
	Was given to her to fly
	To her own place into the desert,
	To a nourishing supply.
	There she was nourished for a season,
	For three and one-half times,
	Away from the face of the Serpent
	With nourishment God designs.*
12:15	But the Serpent spewed out of his mouth
	Water as it wildly roared,
	Working to sweep away the woman
	With the flood that he had poured.
12:16	But the earth worked to help the woman,
	Its mouth being opened wide,
	Drinking the water from the dragon,
	All that he supplied.
12:17	Since the woman escaped his pursuits,
	He was enraged all the more.
	He pursued the rest of her offspring,
	And against them he waged war.
	Now who are the rest of her offspring?
	Those who keep God's commands
	And hold to the witness of Jesus
	And follow what He demands.*

13:1   As the dragon[120] stood on the seashore,
I saw rising from the sea
A beast with ten horns and seven heads
With names of blasphemy.

On each head was a blasphemous name.
On each horn a royal crown,[121]
13:2   And as I looked closer at the beast,*
This is what I found:

Its body resembled a leopard.
Its feet resembled a bear.
Its mouth resembled a lion's mouth,
And arrogance it did air.*

The dragon gave the beast its power,
The one that came from the sea.
He also gave this beast its throne
And great authority.

13:3   Now one of the heads upon this beast
Looked like it had been slain.
But then this mortal wound became healed,
And the whole earth was its gain.

The whole earth was completely amazed
And followed after the beast
Because the fatal wound had been healed.
It amazed, to say the least.*

The Poetic Revelation to John

13:4 So the whole earth worshipped the dragon
Because the beast he worked through,
Giving the beast its authority.
So the beast they worshipped too.

The whole earth said, "Who is like this beast?
There is none that can compare,
And who is able to war with it?
Not one would even dare!"*

13:5 And there was given to it a mouth
Of boasting and blasphemies.
Forty-two months of authority
Was given for it to seize.

13:6 It opened its mouth in blasphemies.
Against God it did rebel.
It blasphemed His name, also His tent
(Those who in heaven dwell).

13:7 Power was given to war with saints
And them to overcome.
Over each tribe, tongue, nation, and clan,
Power was given this one.

13:8 All the people who dwell on the earth
(Just those not in the Lamb's book)
Will render their worship to this beast.
To this beast they all will look.

All those whose names have not been written
In the slain Lamb's book of life
Existing since the world's foundation
Worshipped *to avoid strife.

13:9	If anyone has an ear to hear,
	Listen and do not oppose:
13:10	If anyone captivates others,
	To captivity he goes.

        If any kills by means of the sword,
        By the sword he will be killed.
        Here is the perseverance and faith
        Of the saints to be fulfilled.

13:11	I saw another beast coming up.
	Out of the earth he sprang.
	He had two horns like that of a lamb.
	As a dragon his voice rang.
13:12	All authority from the first beast,
	This beast does exercise
	In the very presence of the beast
	Which from the sea did rise.[122]

        He makes all those who dwell on the earth,
        From the greatest to the least,*
        To worship the one whose wound was healed,
        To worship this first beast.

13:13	Now the second beast performs great signs,
	Calling fire from the skies
	So that it comes down and strikes the earth
	Before man's very eyes.
13:14	He deceives those dwelling on the earth
	By these great signs he released,
	Signs that were given him to perform
	In the presence of the beast.

> He would command those upon the earth
> An image to contrive
> In honor of him slain by the sword
> But who later did revive.

13:15
> He was granted power to give breath
> To the image that was made
> So that the image might even speak,
> Causing all to be afraid.*

> The image would cause the deaths of those
> Who decided to defy.
> The choice was clear for the world to make:
> Worship or you will die.

13:16
> He causes all, the rich and the poor,
> The greatest and the least,
> Those who are free and those who are slaves,
> To receive the mark of the beast.

> The mark was given on their right hand,
> Or their forehead it could be.

13:17
> No one was able to buy or sell
> Without the mark to see.

> Now the mark is the name of the beast.
> It is his number too.

13:18
> Let the one who has understanding
> Calculate with this clue:

> The number of the mark of the beast,
> A human one it will be,
> Namely, six hundred sixty-six,
> Which wisdom will then see.

The Poetic Scriptures of John

14:1   I looked and behold, I saw the Lamb.
On Mount Zion He took His stand
With one hundred forty-four thousand,
Each of them having His brand.

His name was written on their foreheads,
His Father's name written too,
14:2   And then I heard this voice from heaven
Making the sounds these do:

The voice made sounds like rushing waters,
Loud sounds like thunder, I'd say;
But it also sounded like music
That harpists on harps would play.

14:3   They sang a new song before the throne
And before the elders too
And before the four living creatures.
They sang this song that was new.

And no one could learn the song at all.
No one could sing along.*
The one hundred forty-four thousand
Could only sing this song.

These are all those who have been purchased
From the face of the land,[123]
14:4   Those who were not defiled by women,
But who as virgins stand.

> These are the ones who follow the Lamb,
> Wherever He might plan,
> Bought as firstfruits from all mankind
> To God and to the Lamb.

14:5
> And no falsehood was found in their mouth.
> They are blameless in God's sight.
> The one hundred forty-four thousand*
> Sang what none could recite.*

14:6
> Another angel I saw flying
> In the middle of the air
> With an eternal gospel to preach
> To people everywhere.

> The good news came to all those on earth,
> Each nation, tribe, tongue, and clan;

14:7
> "Fear God," he proclaimed in a loud voice,
> "Glorify Him while you can.

> "Since the hour has come for His judgment,
> Worship Him who made all things,
> Who made both the heavens and the earth,
> And the sea and water springs."

14:8
> Another angel, a second one,
> Followed him and announced,
> "Fallen, fallen is Babylon the Great.
> Her judgment has been pronounced.*

> "Fallen, fallen is Babylon the Great,
> She who enticed all nations
> To drink the wine of her awful sins,
> Her raging fornications."

14:9 Then another angel, a third one,
Followed these two and proclaimed
A warning to all about the beast.
In a loud voice he explained:

"Those who worship the beast and image,
And those who his mark receive,
Whether upon their forehead or hand,
Will not get any reprieve.

14:10 "Those will drink of the wine of God's rage
Which is mixed in full measure,
Mixed in the cup of His own wrath,
Receiving His displeasure.

"Those will be eternally tortured
With fire and with brimstone
In the presence of the holy angels
And the Lamb *they had not known.

14:11 "The smoke from their torture will ascend.
Forevermore it will rise.
Neither day nor night will they have rest.
This will be their demise.*

"Those who worship the beast and image,
Who take the mark of his name,
Eternal torture will be their end.
Listen to what I proclaim."*

14:12 Here is the perseverance of saints,
Those who continually hold
To God's commands and faith in Jesus
No matter what may unfold.*

14:13 Then from heaven I heard this command,
"Write!" was a voice's cry.
"Write, 'From now on blessed are the dead,
The ones who in the Lord die.'"

The Spirit replied to what I heard,
"Yes, these are truly blessed,
For following with them are their deeds,
And from their labors they rest."

14:14 I saw someone like a son of man
On a white cloud sitting down.
His hand held a very sharp sickle,
His head a gold victory crown.[124]

14:15 Then from the sanctuary[125] I saw
Another angel; he was loud.
In a tremendous voice he cried out
To him who sat on the cloud:

"Put in your sickle and start to reap,
For the time to reap has come.
Since the harvest on the earth is ripe,
Reap it until it is done."

14:16 The one who sat on the cloud obeyed,
Swinging his sickle to reap,
Gathering the harvest from the earth
As the earth the sickle did sweep.

14:17 Then from the sanctuary[126] in heaven
Another angel came out.
This angel had a sharp sickle too,
Ready to swing it about.

14:18   Another angel came from the altar
            Who over its fire cared.
            To the angel with the sharp sickle
            These orders he then blared:

            "Put in your sickle that is now sharp.
            Over the earth let it swipe,
            And gather the clusters from the vine
            Because her grapes are ripe."

14:19   So the angel swung over the earth
            To gather grapes from its vine,
            And threw them under the wrath of God,
            The great press that makes wine.

14:20   The grapes were trampled in the wine press,
            And out from it did flood,
            Rising up to the horses' bridles,
            For two hundred miles, blood.

15:1   Another sign in heaven I saw,
            Being marvelous and great.
            Seven angels with seven last plagues,
            Completing God's wrathful state.

15:2   I saw what looked like a sea of glass
            That had been mixed with fire,
            And standing there on this sea of glass
            Was a marvelous choir.

The choir were all those who had conquered,
All those who overcame,
Not yielding to the beast or image
Or the number of his name.

15:3 They all were holding harps of God.
This melody they began:
The song of Moses, God's bond slave,
And the song of the Lamb.

"Lord God Almighty, Your works are grand,
Worthy of admiration.
Righteous and genuine are Your ways,
O King of every nation.

15:4 "Since You, O Lord, alone are holy,
Who won't praise Your name?
For all the nations will worship You.
Your right deeds You've made plain."

15:5 After these things I saw in heaven
The tent of witness exposed,
And the sanctuary[127] within it
Was opened up, not closed.

15:6 I also saw the seven angels
Who had the plagues of seven.
Out of the sanctuary they came,
The sanctuary in heaven.

They were clothed with elegant linen.
The linen was bright and clean,
And across the chests of the angels
Bands of gold could be seen.

15:7   And one of the four living creatures
           Gave to the angels to pour
           Seven golden bowls filled with God's wrath,
           God who lives forevermore.

15:8   The sanctuary was filled with smoke,
           Smoke from God's glory and clout.
           None could enter until all the plagues
           Were finished being poured out.

16:1   Then I heard from the sanctuary
           A voice to the angels say,
           "Pour out the seven bowls of God's wrath
           On the earth without delay."*

16:2   And the first angel went and poured
           Into the earth his bowl.
           It was a foul and painful sore
           For the unbelieving soul.*

           The sore did not cause death to occur.
           It only brought great pain
           On those who worshipped the beast's image
           And bore the mark of his name.

16:3   The second angel poured out his bowl.
           In the sea it was applied.
           It became blood as from a dead man,
           And all of the sea life died.

16:4 Then the third angel poured out his bowl
Into the rivers and springs.
All the fresh water became as blood
As judgment on earth's beings.[128]

16:5 I heard the angel of the waters,
"You're righteous, O Holy One,
You who are and who has always been,
For Your judgment has now come.

16:6 "For the blood of some saints and prophets,
On earth they have poured out.
So You have given them blood to drink
Which they deserve, no doubt."

16:7 And I heard these words from the altar:
"Yes! O Lord God," it exclaimed,
"All Your judgments are righteous and true.
The Almighty, You are named."

16:8 And the fourth angel poured out his bowl.
On the sun it was confined,
Which was given the power to scorch
With fire all of mankind.

16:9 As mankind was scorched with intense heat,
The name of God they spurned.
Though He had power over these plagues,
They praised not, nor from sin turned.

16:10 Then the fifth angel poured out his bowl
Upon the throne of the beast.
His kingdom was engulfed in darkness.
All light over them had ceased.*

	They gnawed on their tongues in agony,
16:11	Refusing to repent,
	And they blasphemed the God of heaven
	For the pains and sores He sent.

16:12   The sixth angel poured his bowl upon
Euphrates, the river great.
It dried up for the kings of the east
So they could travel straight.[129]

16:13   Unclean spirits like frogs then came out
From these mouths I could see
Of the false prophet, dragon, and beast,
Spirits numbering three.

16:14   These spirits are demons doing signs.
The world's kings they are for,
To gather them against God Almighty
In the day of God to war.

16:15   ("Behold, like a thief I am coming.
So keep clothed and be awake,
For blessed is the one who stays alert,
And wears the clothes for My sake.

"For all those who do not stay awake
And do not wear My clothes,
Their sinful shame will be viewed by all
Since their deeds I will expose.")*

16:16   And the demons gathered the world's kings,
Bringing them into one place.
In Hebrew it's called Har-Magedon,
Where Almighty God they'll face.

16:17   The seventh angel poured out his bowl.
Upon the air poured this one.
In the sanctuary[130] from the throne,
A loud voice said, "It is done!"

16:18   There were flashes of lightning with sounds.
Peals of thunder formed,
And a great quake like never before
Shook the earth as it stormed.

Never had there been such a quake
Since man came to be on earth.
This was the mightiest and greatest
From the time of mankind's birth.

16:19   The great city was split into three.
The nations' cities fell.
God remembered Babylon the Great,
His wrath on her to shell.

And God gave to Babylon the Great
The full cup of the wine,
Which is the fierceness of His great wrath,
That fell on her at that time.

16:20   And every island just disappeared.
The mountains could not be found.
16:21   Huge hailstones came down from the heavens.
On mankind these stones did pound.

The stones weighed about one hundred pounds.
Men blasphemed God for this hail,
For the plague was extremely severe,
A plague of the greatest scale.

The Poetic Scriptures of John

17:1   Then one of the seven angels came
       (The ones with the seven bowls).
       He spoke with me by saying, "Come here!
       This judgment I will disclose.

       "The one who sits on many waters,
17:2   The great harlot that she's been,
       With whom the earth's kings fornicated,
       Will be judged for her sin.

       "Those who dwell on the earth were made drunk
       With her wine she gave out,
       The wine of her immorality.
       Come see what's coming about."

17:3   He took me away in the Spirit,
       Into a desert place,
       And I saw a woman sitting on
       A beast *with an evil face.

       She was sitting on a scarlet beast.
       Blasphemous names it bore.
       It had seven heads and ten horns.
       Here is what the woman wore:

17:4   The woman wore purple and scarlet
       With gems marvelous and grand,
       Gems of gold, precious stones, and pearls,
       And she held a cup in her hand.

            The cup was gold and filled to the top,
            Full of abominations,
            Full with all kinds of her filthiness,
            Full of her fornications.

17:5   On her forehead a name was written,
            A mystery to me, no less,
            "Babylon the Great, Mother of Harlots
            And of earth's filthiness."

17:6   And I saw the woman drunk with blood,
            Blood that to these belonged,
            The saints and witnesses of Jesus,
            The ones whom she had wronged.*

            As I saw her, I greatly wondered,
17:7   But the angel said to me,
            "Why do you wonder about these things?
            I'll tell you the mystery.

            "Yes, the mystery of the woman,
            This mystery I will tell,
            The seven-headed and ten-horned beast
            Who carries her as well.

17:8   "The beast that you saw was and is not,
            Yet is about to arise,
            Coming up from the bottomless pit,
            But ruin will be its prize.

            "Those who dwell on the earth will marvel
            (Whose names are not in the book
            Existing since the world's foundation).
            To this beast they will look.

"Those whose names aren't in the book of life
Will marvel at this one,
Because this beast, who was and is not,
Was still yet to come.

17:9 "So herein is the mind with wisdom:
The seven heads represent
The seven hills the woman sits on,
17:10 And seven kingdoms[131] are meant.

"Therefore, these are seven kingdoms.
Five have met their demise.
The sixth kingdom is the current one.
The seventh has yet to arise.

"And when the seventh kingdom comes in,
A short time it must remain.
17:11 Now this beast, who was and is not,
Is an eighth one that will reign.

"And this beast is one of the seven,
Yet an eighth one that will reign,
And although this beast will arise,
Destruction will be its gain.

17:12 "Now the ten horns you saw are ten kings
Who have not received power,
But they will receive control as kings
With the beast for one hour.

17:13 "Only one purpose these ten kings serve,
Which is to give their power,
Also to give their authority
To the beast for one hour.

17:14	"They all will wage war against the Lamb, But them the Lamb will defeat, For He's Lord of lords and King of kings. With Him none can compete.*
	"And there in company with the Lamb Are all those whom He called, Those who are chosen and are faithful, Who with the Lamb are enthralled.*
17:15	"The waters on which the harlot sits, To the whole world it alludes. They represent the nations and tongues, Clans and multitudes.
17:16	"The ten horns which you saw and the beast, The harlot they will despise, Making her desolate and naked. Against her these will rise.
17:17	"The harlot's flesh they all will consume, And burn her up with fire, For God has put it into their hearts To execute His desire.
	"For by having a common purpose, They are doing what God willed, Giving their kingdom unto the beast Until God's words are fulfilled.
17:18	"And last of all, the woman you saw," He went on to explain, "She symbolizes the great city Which over earth's kings does reign."

18:1 Next I noticed another angel,
Descending toward the ground.
He came from heaven with great power,
His glory shining around.

The earth was lit up with his glory,
18:2 And with a loud voice he cried,
"Fallen, fallen, is Babylon the Great
Because of what she's supplied.

"She has become a home for demons,
A prison for every kind
Of unclean spirit and hateful bird.
To her they've been assigned.*

18:3 "Fallen, fallen is Babylon the Great,
She who enticed all nations.
They drank the wine of her awful sins,
Her raging fornications.

"And the earth's kings committed with her
Acts of immorality,
And the earth's merchants have become rich
By her sensuality."

18:4 From heaven I heard another voice,
"From her My people I call.
Come out and do not share in her sins
So her plagues on you won't fall.

18:5   "For her sins have piled high as heaven.
God saw her iniquities.
18:6   Pay her back as she gave to others,
And double her penalties.

"In the same cup which was mixed by her,
Mix for her twice her brew.
Pay her back double what she gave out.
Her judgment is now due.*

18:7   "And as she measured out for herself,
Give to her the same degree,
Torment and mourning that's equal to
Her glory and luxury.

"For in her own heart she keeps boasting.
'I sit as a queen,' says she,
'And I am not a helpless widow,
And mourning I'll never see.'

18:8   "For this reason her plagues will arrive
All in one day, *as she's earned,
Pestilence and mourning and famine,
And with fire she'll be burned.

"The Lord God is strong who judges her.
18:9   Judgment the earth's kings will see,
The kings who with her fornicated
And shared in her luxury.

"And they will weep and wail over her.
Out of fear they'll stand afar,
Seeing the smoke rise from her burning
As they see the city char.

18:10 "'Woe!' they will say, 'Woe, the great city,
The strong city, Babylon
Because in just one single hour
Judgment you have drawn.'

18:11 "The earth's merchants weep and mourn for her
Since none can buy their line,
18:12 Cargoes of gold, silver, precious stones,
Pearls, and linen that's fine.

"No one will buy their purple and silk,
Or their scarlet of high price.
They had every kind of citron wood
And ivory merchandise.

"Every article of costly wood,
Of marble, iron, and brass,
They had in their possession to sell,
But all of these things did pass.

18:13 "They had cinnamon, spice, and incense,
Frankincense, perfume, and wine.
They also had cattle, sheep, and wheat,
And flour that is fine.

"They had horses too and chariots,
Humans to be enslaved.
18:14 But all the fruit has vanished from you
Which you've desired and craved.

"And all the things have vanished from you
That were expensive and fine.
No longer will anyone find them,
Burned in one hour's time.[132]

18:15	"The merchants who became rich from her,
	Out of fear they'll stand afar.
	They'll weep and wail over her judgment
	As they see the city char.
18:16	"'Woe!' they will say, 'Woe, the great city,
	Who was a sight to behold,
	Clothed with silk and purple and scarlet,
	Decked with pearls, gems, and gold.'
	"'Woe!' they will say, 'Woe, the great city
	Whom the earth's kings embraced,
18:17	For in one hour all her great wealth
	Has now been brought to waste!'
	"All who get their living by the sea,
	Helmsmen, passengers, sailors,
	Stood from afar as they watched her burn,
18:18	Standing as weepers and wailers.
	"'What is like this great city?' they cried.
18:19	Upon their heads they threw dust.
	They wept and mourned over their losses.
	Wealth from her they did trust.
	"'Woe!' they will say, 'Woe, the great city
	Who from her wealth was earned
	By having their ships at her sea ports,
	For in one hour she has burned!'
18:20	"So rejoice, O heaven, over her,
	Apostles, prophets, and saints
	Because for you God has brought on her
	A judgment *with no restraints."

18:21	A strong angel picked up a boulder
	Like a gigantic millstone.
	He hurled it into the sea and said,
	"Thus Babylon will be thrown.
	"With violence she will be thrown down,
	And will be no longer found.
18:22	Musicians, harpists, flutists, trumpeters,
	From these there'll be no sound.
	"And craftsmen of any kind of craft,
	In you will not be found;
	And the mills that were always busy,
	From these there'll be no sound.
18:23	"And lamps will no longer shine in you,
	You whom the world preferred.*
	The voice of the bridegroom and his bride
	In you will never be heard.
	"For your merchants were the world's great men,
	All nations deceived by your spell.
18:24	You have blood found from prophets and saints,
	And from others you killed as well."

19:1	After these things I heard a great noise
	In heaven from a great crowd.
	They were giving praises to the Lord
	In a voice that sounded loud.

	"Salvation and glory and power
	Belong to our God," they roared,
19:2	"For His judgments are true and righteous.
	Hallelujah! Praise the Lord!"[133]

        "For our God has judged the great harlot
        Who, by her fornications,
        Corrupted all those throughout the earth,
        Corrupted all the nations.

        "The blood of His bond slaves He's avenged."
19:3   Then a second time they roared,
        "Her smoke rises up forevermore.
        Hallelujah! *Praise the Lord!"

19:4   The twenty-four elders fell facedown,
        Worshipping God on the throne,
        Saying with the four living creatures,
        "Amen! Praise the Lord *alone!"[134]

19:5   I heard a voice command from the throne,
        "Give praise to our God you all,
        You His bond slaves, and you who fear Him,
        You who are great and small."

19:6   I heard something like a great crowd's voice,
        Like rushing waters that roar,
        And like the noise that thunder creates
        In a mighty downpour.*

        They said, "Hallelujah! Our God reigns,
        The Lord, the Omnipotent.
19:7   Let us rejoice and be very glad,
        And praises to Him present.

"For the marriage of the Lamb has come.
It has arrived and is here!
His bride has prepared herself for Him,
Waiting for Him to appear."*

19:8 And clothing was given to the bride,
Fine linen, clean and bright
(Which are the righteous acts of the saints),
And she dressed herself in white.

19:9 The angel then turned and spoke to me,
"Write these words," he incited.
"'Concerning the Lamb's marriage supper,
Blessed are all those invited.'

"These are true words from God," he said,
19:10 Then at his feet I dropped.
Starting to worship him, he then said,
"This worship must be stopped!

"I am a fellow servant of yours
And of your brothers too
Who hold to the witness of Jesus.
Worship to me is not due.*

"For the testimony of Jesus
Is the spirit of prophecy.
I am God's angelic messenger.
Give worship to God, not me."

19:11 Next I saw heaven being opened.
A white horse stood in the heights.
Its rider is called Faithful and True.
Rightly He judges and fights.

The Poetic Revelation to John

19:12   His eyes are like a flame of fire.
Royal crowns[135] crowded His head.
He had a name written upon Him,
A name that could not be read.

No one knows the name that was written.
This just the rider could claim.
19:13   He's clothed with a robe that's dipped in blood.
The Word of God is His name.

19:14   Now the armies, which are in heaven,
On white horses followed behind,
Clothed with garments both white and clean
From linen of the best kind.

19:15   And from His mouth comes a sharp long sword
With which the nations He'll smite,
And He'll rule them with an iron rod
So wrong won't prevail, but right.*

The Almighty's wine press of God's wrath,
His fierce wrath, He does tread.
19:16   The words, "King of kings and Lord of lords,"
On His robe and thigh could be read.

19:17   And then I saw standing in the sun
An angel crying out
To all the birds flying in midair.
With a loud voice he did shout:

"Come and gather for God's great supper
19:18   That you may eat the flesh
Of kings, commanders, and mighty men.
Their carcasses will be fresh.*

"Come eat the flesh of all of mankind,
Of free men and of slaves.
Come eat the flesh of the small and great,
Your stomachs being their graves."*

19:19 I saw the earth's kings and their armies
Gathered with the beast to fight,
To battle the Rider and His army,
The One on the horse of white.[136]

19:20 The beast was seized with the false prophet
Who performed signs in his sight,
Signs that deceived those with the beast's mark,
Whose image was their delight.

The beast was thrown with the false prophet
Into the fire alive,
The lake of fire, which burns with brimstone,
And the rest did not survive.

19:21 All others were killed with the long sword
That from His mouth did protrude,
And all the birds were filled with their flesh.
The armies became their food.*

20:1 Then I saw coming down from heaven
With a great chain in his hand,
An angel holding the key to the pit
(The bottomless one, understand).

20:2 The angel then pursued the dragon
Who is the Serpent of old,
Also called the Devil and Satan,
Of whom he grabbed a hold.

20:3 He chained Satan for a thousand years,
Throwing him into the pit.
Shut the lid. Set a seal over him
So no one could open it.*

He could deceive the nations no more
'Til the thousand years were complete,
But at that moment he must be freed
For a short time of deceit.

20:4 I saw thrones and they sat upon them.
Judgment given to them all.
I saw the lives of those beheaded
In answer to God's call.*

These died for the witness of Jesus
And for God's word, which is true,
For refusing to worship the beast
And the beastly image too.

Although there was great persecution,*
The word of God was their stand.
These died for not receiving the mark
On their forehead or their hand.

There came to life all those whom I saw,
And with Christ they did reign.
They ruled with Him for a thousand years,
The world being their domain.*

20:5 The rest of the dead came not to life
'Til the thousand years had passed.
The first resurrection had occurred.
The second would be the last.*

20:6 All those of the first resurrection,
Blessed and holy are they.
The second death, *which is yet to come,
Over them holds no sway.

They all will be priests of God and Christ.
For a thousand years they'll reign,
20:7 And when the thousand years are complete,
Off will come Satan's chain.

From his prison Satan will be freed.
20:8 He will come out to deceive
The nations in the earth's four corners.
Gog and Magog he'll retrieve.

The numbers of them will be so great
As he gathers them for war,
As numerous as the grains of sand
That lie upon the seashore.

20:9 They marched across the breadth of the earth.
The city they encased,
The beloved city where the saints camp,
But fire from heaven raced.

The fire consumed all those who marched,
20:10 But the Devil he was thrown.
He who deceived them was tossed into
The lake of fire and brimstone.

The Poetic Revelation to John

              The beast and false prophet are there too.
              Together they all will be,
              And they'll be tormented day and night
              Forever eternally.

20:11   I saw a throne that was great and white,
              And Him who was seated there.
              Earth and heaven fled from His presence,
              Vanishing into the air.

20:12   I saw the dead, the great and the small,
              Standing before the throne.
              Books were opened and the book of life.
              Their deeds were to be shown.

              They were judged according to their deeds.
              From the books all would be told.
20:13   The sea, death, and Hades surrendered
              All the dead which they did hold.

20:14   The lake of fire is the second death,
              And this is where were bound
20:15   Death and Hades and all those whose names
              Who in life's book aren't found.

21:1   Then a new heaven and a new earth
              Was the next sight given me.
              The first heaven and earth had vanished,
              And there is no more sea.

21:2   The holy city, new Jerusalem,
           I watched as she began
           Coming down out of heaven from God
           Like a bride dressed for her man.

21:3   I heard from the throne a loud voice say,
           "God's tent is with men! See!
           And God Himself will dwell among them,
           And His people they will be.

21:4   "He will wipe every tear from their eyes.
           Death will forever be gone.
           No one will mourn, cry, or agonize.
           The first things have all passed on."

21:5   And He who sits on the throne then said,
           "See! I make all things new!"
           Then He told me, "Write for this reason:
           These words are faithful and true."

21:6   And He said to me, "It is finished!"
           Then these words He did append:
           "I'm the Alpha and the Omega,
           The Beginning and the End.

           "I'll give freely, to the one who thirsts,
           From the water of life's springs.
21:7   I'll be his God, and he'll be My son.
           The victor inherits these things.

21:8   "But not so for the unbelieving,
           The cowards and the base,
           The murderers, the idolaters,
           And those who to witchcraft race.

> "Yes, not so for the unbelieving,
> The immoral and the liar
> Since all of those with sinful lifestyles
> Will inherit the lake of fire.
>
> "With fire and brimstone this lake burns.
> Its fire will never cease.[137]
> It's the second death of the sinful.
> They will not rest in peace."*

21:9 One of the seven angels who had
One of the bowls of wrath
(Those that contained the seven last plagues),
He came into my path.

He said, "Come here, and I will show you
The wife of the Lamb, His bride."
21:10 He swept me away in the Spirit,
This angel being my guide.

We came to a mountain great and high.
He showed me a certain town,
The holy city, Jerusalem,
From God's heaven coming down.

21:11 How she shined with the glory of God!
Her brilliance was like a stone,
As costly as crystal-clear jasper.
Through her God's glory was shown.*

21:12 She possessed a wall, both wide and high,
And within it were twelve gates.
At each of these there was an angel.
(Twelve angels this equates.)

And there I saw on each of the gates
The name of a certain tribe.
Twelve names of the sons of Israel
Had been written *by a scribe.

21:13 There were three gates facing east and north,
And three gates in the south wall.
There were also three gates facing west,
Which makes twelve gates in all.*

21:14 The city's wall had foundation stones
(Twelve of them was my count)
With the Lamb's apostles' names on them.
Twelve names was that amount.

21:15 And the angel who had talked with me
Possessed a golden reed
To measure the city, its gates and wall.
To measure he did proceed.

21:16 The city is laid out as a square.
It's as long as it is wide.
He measured the city with the reed,
Measuring every side.

It is fourteen hundred miles in length,
Its width and height as well.
21:17 The wall was measured in cubit lengths.
Its height I now will tell.*

One hundred forty-four cubits high,
That was the angel's call.
Human measurements the angel used
In measuring the wall.

21:18	Now the wall was made out of jasper,
	And the city was a gold mass,
	Not alloyed* gold but completely pure,
	As pure as crystal-clear glass.
21:19	And the city wall's foundation stones
	Were dressed with every gem.
	From the first foundation to the twelfth
	Will be the order of them:
	Jasper, sapphire, and chalcedony
	(A foundation for each gem),*
21:20	Emerald, sardonyx, and sardius,
	That's the first half of them.*
	Chrysolite and beryl and topaz
	(A foundation for each gem),*
	Chrysoprase, jacinth, and amethyst,
	That's the last half of them.*
21:21	Of twelve pearls the twelve gates were made,
	One pearl for every gate.
	The street of the city was pure gold.
	Like clear glass it did radiate.
21:22	Not one sanctuary[138] did I see
	In this city that was new,
	For its sanctuary is the Lamb,
	The Lord God Almighty too.
21:23	The city has no need for the sun
	Or the moon to be its light,
	For the Lamb is the lamp of the city
	Through which God's glory shines bright.

21:24	The earth's kings will bring their glory there.
	The nations will walk by its light.
21:25	Its gates will never close in the day,
	For there will never be night.
21:26	The nations will bring their glory there
	And bring their honor too.
21:27	Nothing unclean will enter its gates.
	No, it will never get through.*

        And none who practice filth and deceit
        Can enter because of sin.
        The Lamb's book of life has all the names
        Of those who can enter in.

22:1	Coming out from God's throne and the Lamb's,
	The angel to me then showed
	A river of the water of life.
	As clear as crystal it flowed.
22:2	The river flowed throughout the city
	Down the middle of its street,
	And on either side of the river
	Was the tree of life to eat.

        The tree of life bore twelve kinds of fruit,
        One for each month of the year.
        The leaves brought healing to all nations.
22:3   The curse will never be here.

In the city God's throne and the Lamb's
Forevermore will be,
And the bond slaves of God will serve Him.

22:4   His face they will always see.

God's name will be upon their foreheads.

22:5   No longer will there be night.
They'll have no need for lamps or the sun.
The Lord God will be their light.

They will be illumined by the Lord,
And they'll reign forevermore.

22:6   He said, "These words are faithful and true."
(The same words God said before.)[139]

The Lord, God of the prophets' spirits,
His angel He did entrust
To show His bond slaves these events,
And come suddenly they must.[140]

22:7   ("Behold, I am coming suddenly.
Always be watchful and look.*
Blessed is the one who obeys the words
Of the prophecy of this book.")

22:8   My name is John, and I've heard and seen
This divine revelation.
After seeing and hearing all this,
I fell down in admiration.

I began to worship at the feet
Of the angel whom God sent,

22:9   But he said, "I'm your fellow servant.
Stop this and repent.

"I'm a fellow servant of prophets
And of your brothers too,
Of all who heed the words of this book.
The worship of God pursue.

22:10 "Do not seal up the prophetic words
That you have written here,
But preserve this book for all to read,
For the time is very near.[141]

22:11 "Let the one who practices wrong
Go on practicing sin,
And let the one who practices filth
Be just as he has been.

"Let the one who's considered righteous
Continue to practice right,
And let the one who is set apart[142]
Live holy in God's sight."

22:12 "Behold!" the Lord Jesus then proclaimed,
"Suddenly,[143] I will come.
My reward I'll give to every man
According to what he's done.

22:13 "I'm the Alpha and the Omega,
The First One and the Last.
I am the Beginning and the End.
To Me all should hold fast.*

22:14 "How blessed are all those who wash their robes
That they may have the right
To enter the city by its gates
And eat from life's tree in delight.

22:15 "Outside are the dogs, and sorcerers,
And those who fornicate,
Murderers, idolaters, liars,
All those in a sinful state.

22:16 "I, Jesus, have sent you My angel
To reveal to you this word
To tell to the churches what must be,
Which is what you've seen and heard.

"I am David's root and his offspring.
I'm the bright, morning star.
22:17 The Spirit and the bride call out, 'Come!'
To listeners near and far.[144]

"The one who is thirsty let him come,
And all who wish to receive
From the water of life without cost,
Let him come and believe.

22:18 "I testify to each one who hears
The prophecies in this book.
Don't take away and don't add to them.
This God can't overlook.

"To the one who adds, God too will add,
The plagues written in this book.
22:19 To the one who subtracts, God will too,
Since to Him they do not look.*

"God will from him take away his part
From life's tree *that was described,
And his part from the holy city
Which in this book is inscribed.

22:20 "The One who gives this testimony,
The Lord Jesus, I am He.*
I declare I am truly coming,
And I'm coming suddenly."[145]

Yes, come, Lord Jesus, as You have said.
Yes, come and return again.
22:21 The grace of the Lord is with all saints!
Come, Lord Jesus! Amen.

ENDNOTES

1. Implied, the darkness cannot keep the light from shining.
2. Literally, *through Jesus Christ*.
3. Some manuscripts read *God*; others read *Son*. Jesus certainly is both God's Son and God (see verse 1).
4. Implied since God used John to reveal Jesus.
5. Note the quotes. John quotes God's testimony first in verse 33 before giving his testimony in verse 34.
6. Literally, *the tenth hour*. John does not tell us if he used the Jewish method or Roman method of telling time. John wrote at the close of the century and his audience was primarily non-Jewish; therefore, he used the Roman method of time.
7. John does not tell us the meaning of Peter's name but assumes the reader has that knowledge from Matthew 16:18.
8. The poetic description used to refer to the person the prophets prophesied would come.
9. Jesus is most certainly alluding to Genesis 28:12.
10. The Greek may mean *again* or *above*. Nicodemus thought He meant *born again*, but Jesus goes on to explain that He meant *born from above*. Since the English word *anew* can mean *again* or *in a new way*, it is used here.
11. The gospel does not state that the wind was blowing. Jesus used living illustrations. In John 15 He was probably going through a vineyard when using the vine to illustrate spiritual truth. Here the wind is that living illustration.
12. Literally, *Truly, truly*.
13. Most versions read *only begotten*. The Greek word does not come from the word *begot* but from the word *become*. Thus, the emphasis is on the uniqueness of the Son's existence.
14. Literally, *He had to go through Samaria*. It was not uncommon for the Jews to travel a longer route to avoid Samaria. Great religious tension existed between them.

15. Derived from Genesis 48:21, 22.
16. Literally, *about the sixth hour*. See John 1:39 notes.
17. Literally, *the seventh hour*. See John 1:39 notes.
18. Literally, *Jesus*.
19. Literally, *the Father*.
20. Literally, *the Scriptures*.
21. These Jews knew the Scriptures very well and had much of it memorized word for word.
22. Literally, *two hundred denarii*. A denarius was one day's pay for a common laborer.
23. Literally, *Truly, truly, I say to you*.
24. Derived from Jesus's words, *Truly, truly*.
25. *Christ, the Messiah* is not used by John here, although these are terms used to refer to the Holy One.
26. Literally, *the Jews*, which in this case refers to the religious leaders.
27. Derived from Leviticus 23:34.
28. The word *circumcise* literally means *to cut around*. Jesus is contrasting their cutting with His healing and their focus on one part of the body with His focus on the entire person.
29. Three times in this chapter Jesus is claiming to be the I Am of Exodus 3:14 (verses 28 and 58 and here). The same Greek construction is in all three of these verses.
30. Same Greek construction as verse 24 and verse 58.
31. This group is different than those who had faith. The Greek uses a prepositional phrase with the word *believe* to describe faith (*believe in Him*) as in verse 30. But in this verse that preposition is not in the Greek, although some translations insert one. As we read on we note that Jesus accuses this group of belonging to the Devil, which obviously means their belief falls short of saving faith.
32. Literally, *I Am*. See 8:24 notes.
33. This is not stated. John assumes the reader knows this.
34. This is added information; John's readers would have known that Solomon's portico was sheltered and a popular gathering place at this time of year.
35. The Greek word for *love* in this verse (*phileo*) refers to a friendship. In verse 5, John uses another Greek word for love, *agapao*, which emphasizes a decision to sacrifice for the good of another.
36. The meaning of the name *Didymus*.
37. Poetic elaboration. Jesus was disturbed by these mourners who were not mourning in their hearts but putting on an act.
38. The ancient pound was twelve ounces.
39. Literally, *three hundred denarii*. A denarius was one day's pay for a common laborer.

40 Poetic elaboration. These Greeks had abandoned their pagan beliefs and embraced the God of Israel as the one true God.
41 John does not say from where Satan will be cast out. This information is from Revelation 12:7-12.
42 Literally, *Truly, truly, I say to you*.
43 Derived from the context of Psalm 41.
44 Same Greek construction as John 8:24. See the notes there.
45 John does not name the feast here.
46 The Greek word is *agapao*. See 11:3 note. The unselfish nature of this love is stressed in this chapter and the next. It is not consistently translated this way in the poetry. Sometimes it is translated as *really love* as in verse 23.
47 Most versions read, *already clean*. The Greek word is the noun form of the verb *prune* in verse 2. This is an obvious play on words.
48 Derived from 1:18 and 14:9.
49 Literally, *Truly, truly, I say to you*.
50 This is the Greek word, *phileo*, which refers to the love between friends. See 11:3 notes.
51 This is the Greek word *phileo*.
52 This can be a question or a statement.
53 The word, *know* in the Greek text stresses a personal knowledge. Eternal life is defined here as a personal relationship with the Lord.
54 A word meaning truly.
55 The same Greek construction in 8:24, 28, 58; 13:19. See 8:24 notes.
56 Derived from 12:32.
57 The Greek word for *Pavement* is a compound word with one of the words being *stone*.
58 Literally, *the sixth hour*.
59 Derived from Matthew 27:37.
60 The context of Psalm 22.
61 Derived from 18:11.
62 Derived from 3:1,2.
63 *God and Lord* is derived from Thomas's confession in verse 28.
64 The Greek word is *agapao*, which is a love of sacrifice. Peter answers with a different word for love, *phileo*, which refers to a friendship. See 11:3 note.
65 Translations read, *more than these*. It is not clear what Jesus wanted Peter to compare his love to.
66 Poetic elaboration. Note that this is a different question than the first one. Jesus is not asking Peter to compare his love for Him to anything. He is asking Peter straight out if he loves Him unselfishly (agapao). Peter replies with a different word for love, phileo, which refers to friendship.

67 Jesus takes Peter's answer of friendship (phileo) and asks him if he loves Him as a friend. This time Peter answers the question with the same word for love that Jesus had in His question (phileo).
68 Derived from John 1:1.
69 The remaining lines in this stanza elaborate on the meaning of *advocate*.
70 The Greek word, commonly translated as *atoning sacrifice* or *propitiation*, refers to a sin payment that satisfies God's wrath upon sin.
71 John is referring to the new commandment Christ gave in John 13:34, to love one another as Christ loved us.
72 Derived from John 13:34.
73 The emphasis of the word *know* in this letter is a personal relationship. See John 17:3 notes.
74 Literally, *the evil one*.
75 Literally, *children*.
76 The Greek word is *agapao*, which refers to an unselfish love that focuses on the good of another. In the remainder of this letter this word will be described as an unselfish or selfless love without being footnoted.
77 Literally, *Jesus Christ*.
78 The word is usually translated *know* but refers to a personal knowledge.
79 See 2:13 note for the word *know* here and in verse 8.
80 See 4:2 note.
81 Poetic elaboration. John is possibly referring to the unforgivable sin of which Jesus spoke in Matthew 12:31.
82 Literally, *the evil one*.
83 See 4:2 note.
84 Literally, *paper and black ink*.
85 Literally, *black ink and a reed*.
86 The Greek word may mean *soon* or *suddenly*. There are unfulfilled events in this prophetic book, such as the second coming of Christ, which was not soon to the immediate readers. Therefore, *suddenly* has been chosen as the translation.
87 The time when the first of these events come to pass.
88 The Greek word is agapao, which refers to an unselfish love that focuses on the good of another.
89 The Greek word may mean a spiritual being that is God's messenger (i.e., an angel) or a human being that is God's messenger like John the Baptist in Mark 1:2. The letters were written to human beings.
90 The remaining lines in this stanza are poetic elaboration. This pattern is followed in each address to the seven churches.
91 Poetic elaboration on what it means to hear. This pattern is followed for the ending of all the letters to the seven churches.
92 There are two Greek words translated as *crown*. One refers to a kingly crown (*diadema*) and the other refers to a victory wreath (*stephanos*). This Greek word is a victory wreath.

93   The Greek word may mean *soon* or *suddenly*.
94   Manna was white. See Exodus 16:31.
95   See 1:5 note.
96   Derived from 1:4.
97   The Greek word may mean *soon* or *suddenly*.
98   The Greeks had the same word for *take* and *receive*. The picture here is of God giving crowns, which were meant for one, to someone else.
99   A victory wreath. See 2:10 notes.
100 The meaning of *amen* is *truth*.
101 The Greek word may mean *ruler*, as in Ephesians 3:10, or *beginning*.
102 The Greek word for *love* here is phileo, which is affectionate love.
103 These are victory wreaths. See 2:10 notes.
104 Derived from verse 2.
105 The Greek word may mean *come* or *go*. Since the horses go out in response to this command, *go* seems to be the meaning here and in verses 3, 5, and 7.
106 See 2:10 notes.
107 *dearth* is another word for famine.
108 If there were four methods of death, one would expect the same preposition to be used for all four in the Greek text—*kill with sword, with dearth, with plagues, and with wild beasts*. But the preposition changes in the Greek to *by wild beasts*, which could define how the plagues were carried.
109 Derived from 5:5, 6.
110 Derived from verse 11.
111 These are victory wreaths. See 2:10 notes.
112 The Greek word refers to the inner part of the temple, the Holy of Holies.
113 Some versions translate as *nations*, which here refer to the unbelieving world.
114 The bottomless pit.
115 The Greek word may mean *soon* or *suddenly*.
116 *Christ* means *Anointed One*, and He is the final king of Israel.
117 See 11:1 notes.
118 The Greek word refers to a victory wreath as opposed to a kingly crown. See 2:10 notes.
119 The Greek word refers to a kingly crown. This is in contrast to the woman's victory wreath. See 2:10 notes.
120 Some Greek copies of Revelation have *I stood*, referring to John, instead of *he stood*, referring to the dragon.
121 See 12:3 note.
122 Derived from verse 1.
123 Literally, *from the earth*.
124 A victory wreath. See 2:10 notes.
125 See 11:1 notes.

126 See 11:1 notes.
127 See 11:1 notes. *sanctuary* is also in 15:6, 8; 16:1.
128 Derived from the next verse.
129 Poetic elaboration. The kings would not have to travel around the river as they would normally do. See a map.
130 See 11:1 notes.
131 Most translations say *kings*. Daniel 7:17, 23 uses the words *kings* and *kingdoms* interchangeably. Here in Revelation John knew of only six kingdoms, the sixth being the Roman Empire. However, he knew of many more kings of Rome.
132 Derived from verse 19.
133 *Hallelujah* means *Praise the Lord*. See also the next verses.
134 Literally, *Amen! Hallelujah.*
135 See 12:3 note.
136 Derived from verse 11.
137 Derived from Revelation 20:10.
138 See 11:1 notes.
139 Derived from Revelation 21:5.
140 See 1:1 notes.
141 See 1:3 notes.
142 *set apart* is the meaning of the word *holy*.
143 See 1:1 notes.
144 Poetic elaboration. There is disagreement over whether Jesus is speaking in verses 17 to 19 or John.
145 See 1:1 notes.

www.ingramcontent.com/pod-product-compliance
Lightning Source LLC
Chambersburg PA
CBHW021057080526
44587CB00010B/284